WRITE

with

INTENTION

A Mindful Journey to Writing Your Book

by Charlotte Chipperfield

Her Narrative

Cover design by Jennifer Ann Birge

To protect the privacy of the individuals mentioned in this book, names and identifying characteristics have been changed.

Publisher's Cataloging-in-Publication Data
Names: Chipperfield, Charlotte.

Title: Write with intention : a mindful journey to writing your book / Charlotte Chipperfield.

Description: Wilmington, DE : Her Narrative, 2025. | Summary: Covers how to write a book from idea conception through publication and marketing. Also covers developing a writer's mindset and growing as an individual in the process, including dealing with self-doubt, procrastination, and writer's block.

Identifiers: LCCN 2025916178 | ISBN 9798999540799 (hardcover) | ISBN 9798999540744 (pbk.) | ISBN 9798999540720 (ebook) | ISBN 9798999540706 (audio book)

Subjects: LCSH: Authorship. | Creation (Literary, artistic, etc.). | Publishers and publishing. | BISAC: LANGUAGE ARTS & DISCIPLINES / Writing / Authorship. | LANGUAGE ARTS & DISCIPLINES / Writing / Business Aspects. | LANGUAGE ARTS & DISCIPLINES / Writing / General.

Classification: LCC PN147.C45 2025 | DDC 808.02--dc23

LC record available at https://lccn.loc.gov/2025916178

Dedication

To anyone who has ever considered
putting their story on the page:

Your voice matters. Your story matters.

Contents

Introduction

If you have ever had a spark, an urge, or a quiet calling to write your stories, ideas, and wisdom into a book, you've arrived at the right place. Storytelling is a form of empowerment, healing, and self-definition. To claim your voice unapologetically in a world that prefers us to whisper is one of the bravest acts you can take. When we stop asking for permission and start living and creating on our terms, our immediate world—along with the wider world around us—can expand in new and beautiful ways.

Writing is an act of deepening relationships with both ourselves and the world. When we tell our authentic stories—be it through fiction or nonfiction—from our truest selves, we build a bridge for connection with communities of readers. Your story has the ability to create a positive impact for the reader; it unlocks something bigger than the words on the page. Writing offers a portal into new worlds, ideas, and concepts.

But what if the secret to writing an impactful book isn't found in more effort but in slowing down to listen to your true intention? Just as a slingshot needs to be pulled back before it can spring forward, taking the time to intentionally assess what you want to accomplish with your writing before diving into the details of *how* you're going to write can both deepen your writing experience and allow for more ease as you reach for your writing goals.

According to author Joseph Epstein, who wrote in *The New York Times*, "81 percent of Americans feel they have a book in them—and that they should write it."[1] Of those 81 percent, very few end up publishing a book. The two reasons why someone doesn't finish writing their book are attributed to a lack of know-how and self-doubt. This statistic makes me believe that the world is missing out on too many amazing stories. As writers starting out, there is so much we just don't know. We have to develop a belief in our stories along with what is possible for ourselves. This combination of developing both writing skills and a writing mindset is what this book aims to achieve because you are worthy of engaging with your creativity in the form of writing.

Creating is a natural state of being human. It is also a place to deepen our relationship to our emotions and beliefs. If you dream of writing a book, it is about deciding what you want and going for it. The caveat is that you have to be willing to embark on the whole journey and not solely focus on the end result of being published. Your worth is not determined by how much you push through the writing process, so why not make it as enjoyable as possible? The journey of writing a book begins by asking the questions: Who do you need to become to have your book in the world? What do you have to be, do, and believe to fully arrive at your success?

By taking the time to create the space to establish a strong writing foundation, you can spring forward with greater clarity and more confidence. By taking the time to get clear on *why* you are writing the book, creating an outline, establishing a consistent writing practice, and being accountable, your book can be written and published.

This book will support you in doing just that. It will help you tap into your heart, mind, and soul to create an intentional and impactful book tied to your legacy. This is a safe space to explore your creativity and writing to set you up for success with less guesswork and with strong consideration for nurturing yourself along the writing journey—a piece I often see omitted in standard writing advice. There rarely seems to be any consideration for the *person* writing the book. Writing with intention means being willing to explore the many ways in which you can choose to reach your writing goals. Throughout your writing journey, do you want to experience stress, worry, and anxiety? Or do you want to experience flow and ease?

The craft of writing is a practice that is continually explored as long as you write. This isn't about writing a book in a specific amount of time. The length of time it takes to develop your writing skills is irrelevant. The time it takes to write your book *is* the time it takes to write your book. It could take decades or one year. The length of time it takes to write your book does not indicate the quality of writer that you are.

How to Use This Book

This book is for writers at any stage of the writing process. Maybe you're a beginner just getting started, or maybe you have been dabbling in writing for a while. Maybe you're a writer with a published book, but you didn't enjoy the process the first time around and want to do it differently next time. No matter where you are on the writing journey, whether you are writing fiction or nonfiction, if you are open to an expansive writing experience, this book will support you in creating a joyful writing journey that helps you achieve your goals.

To get the most out of this book, I recommend initially reading this book in its entirety. Then, you can use it as a reference to come back to at any point along the writing journey. The first few chapters explore the mindset and core foundational pieces that many writers skip over, which results in never completing a book. The second grouping of chapters will focus on providing practical tips to help you implement what you are learning. It is one thing to have the knowledge; it is another to take action. I aim to provide you with the tools and information you need as a springboard to help you build writing momentum.

Everyone has a story. There is a place for your story on the shelves. It is a matter of being brave enough to tell your story and do the work required to see it come to life. Just because something is challenging doesn't mean it isn't worth doing. If you bring to mind some of your favorite songs, they resonate with you for a reason. Let your book do the same for your readers.

Writing a book is like training and preparing for a marathon. It hurts like hell at first, but then, training session by training session, you get stronger, better, and can go farther. The key is that you must keep showing up. Giving up after mile one isn't going to get you to the finish line. You have to keep improving even when it's uncomfortable and you want to give up. Stretching our capacity isn't comfortable, but if we keep going, we'll find that the discomfort is temporary, which eventually gives way to an expanded creative possibility. Nothing beats the feeling of crossing the finish line knowing you gave it your all.

It can be scary to find out what's on the other side of your creative potential. Let's find out together.

Why Writing with Intention Matters

Every book begins not with words, but with intention. As an author embarking on the journey of writing a book, your intention not only fulfills a personal desire to tap into your creativity, but it also defines an experience for your readers. Being intentional with writing a book means that you understand *why* you are writing the book. A book is not food for the ego, but rather an opportunity to capture your ideas and leave a positive imprint in the world.

Your intention for writing a book paves an expansive path for readers to travel down by entertaining them, teaching them, inspiring them, and potentially planting seeds for changes in their own lives. The intention behind writing a book starts with recognizing whether your primary motivation is to say that you've written a book or to have the courage to let the creative journey unfold. When you have the courage to let the creative journey unfold, you allow yourself to become the person you need to become, which leads to you having a book in the world.

For many writers, there is a soul calling to write a book. For some, it is a creative expression. For others, it's a legacy or a way to support their business goals. For some—like me—it's all of the above. If you are hesitant to call yourself an author or a writer, let me ask you this: Are you curious about putting words on the page? If the answer is yes, you are a writer. You've decided to express yourself and your ideas through words. There is no greater definition needed.

In the world of medicine, the word *intention* means "the healing process of a wound."[2] As writers, many times our real-life experiences are woven into the stories we tell, no matter if they are fiction or nonfiction. Our wounds are a part of who we are. The way we earn our scars often holds a powerful story and life lesson. This is why writing can be a healing process, not only for you, but for your readers. Through sharing your experiences, readers can feel seen for who they are and validate their own life experiences. Having clear intentions for why you are writing your book is not just for you. These intentions set the stage for what the reader will take away.

Your reason for writing a book—along with your intentions for the reader—matters because a book is a powerful tool. The French Revolution was started in part because the printing press allowed citizens greater access to information.[3] A book is the bridge that connects ideas and worlds and allows readers to expand their minds. I like to take it a step further by claiming that books can incite ideas which can incite empathy, which can then incite positive change. Books are a way of sharing ideas and can be a catalyst for inspiration and personal change.

I have an endless list of books that have had a great impact on me. There have been spiritual books like Michael A. Singer's *The Untethered Soul: The Journey Beyond Yourself*, which helped me tap into my own power.[4] Building off that, *The Pivot Year: 365 Days To Become The Person You Truly Want To Be* by Brianna Wiest made me feel seen.[5] Memoirs such as *The Glass Castle* by Jeannette Walls have stuck with me.[6] I fell in love with *Book Lovers* by Emily Henry, who not only let me geek out about books while reading a book, but I saw my own fiction writing style reflected back to me.[7] *La Vie, According to Rose* by Lauren Parvizi had me longing to be in Paris again, falling in love, and making soul-aligned big decisions about my life.[8]

Books have the capacity to touch our souls, make us feel a little less alone, and inspire a greater vision for our lives. And think about it, if they can do that on a personal level, just imagine if one hundred or a hundred thousand people read the same book and have a similar experience. That is the power of storytelling. Our brains are literally wired for story, as Lisa Cron explores in her very helpful and inspiring book *Wired for Story*.[9] Even before humans had the written word, verbal stories were shared between communities as a way to pass down cautionary tales and ancestral wisdom.

Our brains remember stories over simple facts because stories have the ability to appeal to all of our senses.

That's why having the poor intention of wanting to write a book in the hopes that it will make millions of dollars will make the writing process that much harder, unsatisfying, and less impactful. Writing with intention not only brings clarity to you as the author, but that intent can be felt through the words that you write. Readers are perceptive and can feel this intent come across on the page. Poor intentions may lead to taking shortcuts when writing, or not even writing the book at all by using a ghostwriter. (No shade to ghostwriters. You hold an important place in this world.) But readers are perceptive; they can tell when something has been created with commercial intent versus through creative means. That's why so many of us hate to see those clickbait-y headlines online. We've fallen for them enough to know that when we click on them, there isn't much of an article to back them up. These were created solely for the clicks to justify the advertisements that pop up on the screen as we try to scroll through the article—it's infuriating! (Please tell me I'm not the only one!) The point is, don't be a clickbait author. Provide your audience with something of substance. Pull them into your world of fantasy, take them on a journey through a time that changed your life, or help them heal a broken heart by falling in love with your romance novel's characters. Connect with your readers, allow them to feel something, and make them think.

If you truly want to have a positive impact, improve other people's lives, and expand as an individual through writing, then it is about embracing all aspects of the writing journey. And while you're at it, why not entertain readers a little too? That's the recipe for an impactful book. This book will help you do that.

I'm the person to guide you through this process—not only because I'm a book coach and editor—but because I know what it is like to have a soul calling to write a book yet hold that book idea inside of you for decades, waiting for the perfect day to write it.

Growing up, I was the kid who was much happier writing and self-publishing my books with a cardboard cover and ribbon binding than playing soccer. When I wasn't doing that, I was reading—and then reenacting *The Box Car Children* in my outdoor hideout built from the natural canopy of interlocking tree branches.[10] Even at an early age, I loved characters. I loved the emotions centered around the sensation of being alive. I loved how emotions could bring characters together. I loved getting insight into how another person lives their life and how they deal with challenges. Take a fiction book, for example. This is the only time we're ever able to get inside the head of another person. It is the only time we're exposed to exactly what they are thinking. We can't do that in real life—we can only assume. That's cool—and trippy. Through nonfiction, we get to explore topics and gain insight that inspires us to take a step or two in the right direction to transform our own lives. As readers, we get to explore the emotions woven into books as well as what is evoked within us in response to what we are reading. While I couldn't articulate all these things as a kid, these reasons remain true today.

As adulthood approached, I embarked on a career in marketing for its storytelling potential. After a decade of grinding my way toward the C-suite, I could feel my soul screaming from the inside for something different and more aligned. This resistance was challenging to understand because I did have opportunities to write. I wrote thousands of social media posts, newsletters, and website copy—so why did I feel so creatively empty? Because if I were being honest, only one percent of my job revolved around writing. The rest was tied up in spreadsheets, troubleshooting data flow, and convincing leadership that marketing held value—and it does. But the reason for my resistance was that there were multiple novels—and this book—brewing inside of me.

The challenge, like many writers, was finding the time. In my twenties and thirties, I was living my best life in San Francisco, and I prioritized my relationships and friendships. Not only did I prioritize social events, but my downtime consisted of lots of reality TV. None of which I regret. I did have times when I would sit down to write, but I often left those writing sessions feeling like everything I wrote was garbage. None of my friends or family members were writing a book, so I didn't have any examples of what the process looked like. I had no clue what was involved in writing a book. I, like many, thought that if you were a real author, writing a book would come easily. How I laugh (with great respect) at my younger self. This book is not only a tool for you to be successful as a writer, but it is a love letter to my younger self. I didn't know what I didn't know. Thankfully, I kept plugging away at writing. With time, I decided to tap into a local writing group to avoid spending another decade click-clacking on my keyboard solo.

Let me tell you—I was shaking in my boots at that basement door leading down to a room full of authors. I could not have been more nervous, strange basement setting aside. As much as I loved writing, I hadn't connected with many writers. I had no idea what I was walking into. What I do know is that my brain assumed that everyone else in the room was a best-selling author and I was an impostor.

That couldn't have been further from the truth. As I started to engage with the group, I realized that everyone was at a different stage along their writing path, and every single one of them was willing to share. What I also learned was that there was so much to learn about the craft of writing—and the more you learn, the stronger a writer you can become. That's why writing your first book is the hardest—the learning curve is large and steep.

Through this newfound commitment to learning about writing, I found myself becoming disenchanted when I learned that there was a formula-like way for writing a book.

I genuinely thought that an author just sat down and let the plot flow. I had no idea that there was a structure that many books and movies follow. Having said that, not all books are the same, but there are helpful guidelines for writing a book that also meets reader expectations, some of which we will explore in this book.

That's why I am here. I'm here to encourage you to get started and keep going. I'm also here to share what you need to know to write a powerful and engaging book. Through all my experiences in life and writing, I know my life's purpose isn't to set up another marketing campaign. My purpose is to hold space for writers to connect with their voice so that they can write, edit, and publish books that inspire and create a positive impact in the world. I know how much power each of our voices holds. For too long, I silenced my voice to please and placate others. I second-guessed myself and my capabilities because I was afraid of this power. When I finally decided to follow my inner calling of writing books, I began to grow and expand in ways that expanded my life. I want that for you too.

Through my own journey of inner work and coming back to what truly lights me up—storytelling and books—I started to engage deeper with the craft of writing. The truth is that writing a book with intention means embarking on a journey of personal development as much as it is about the skill of writing. There will be challenges and the emergence of negative beliefs and self-doubt that require our attention to make the necessary mindset shifts along the writing journey. I don't say that to scare or deter you. It's an act of courage to write a book, and the product is not only a beautiful story, but a beautiful and expanded individual who can proudly stand behind their work, be seen, and share it with the world— when you are ready, of course.

Having a clear intention will guide you through the writing process and beyond. Take, for example, the process of trying out a new recipe from a five-star restaurant's cookbook. Would you just grab all the ingredients and toss them together, hoping you achieve the final product? Or would you take the time to intentionally follow each step of the recipe? By choosing to follow each step, you may learn a new cooking tip or technique as you create a satisfying meal. By taking the time to intentionally invest in the process, you enjoy eating the final meal. The alternative cooking method of tossing it all together in the hope that it will turn into dinner is a total disappointment. There is nothing worse than wasting your time cooking a recipe—or writing a book—that turns out to be a disappointment.

All great things begin with a clear intention. This is essential to your writing process. It's time to lay your foundation for why you are writing a book so that your voice can be heard and readers will listen.

Words hold immense power—both the ones we say to ourselves and the ones we write—and it's time to share yours. Together, we will unapologetically and intentionally write your book. Having clarity around your why for writing your book is important. It's a powerful and fulfilling process filled with integrity and purpose. It comes with many rewards, but most importantly, it comes with the responsibility to own your story to allow others to feel seen. When we can hold the space for our creative expression through words, we can become a channel for meaning. So, dear writer, knowing the power that a story holds, what is your intention for writing your story?

2

The Creative Process

Creativity is a powerful force that lives within each of us. In essence, it is the truest expression of who we are—at least in that moment of time. Creativity is a flowing force that invites us to express a story, an emotion, an idea, an image, a song, or a baked good that reflects a particular period in our lives. What I love about creativity is that it's ever flowing. It's a natural state and is never stagnant. Much like a surfer chooses which wave to ride, we get to choose how we ride our creativity.

The challenge for many of us—myself included—is that we've fallen for the societal expectation that we must always be productive. We must always be working toward a goal that will have a financial payoff. It is no wonder so many people are starved for the opportunity to express themselves creatively. When was the last time you allowed yourself to be truly creative without the expectation of the outcome or payout?

I meet lots of writers who are seeking a creative outlet. However, so much of our days revolve around what we can achieve or produce in order to earn for ourselves and our employers. We hop from one metric to the other and insist that they become bigger, bolder, and more "productive" month-over-month. While work is a part of life and we all need to earn money to live, it doesn't mean that every moment of our lives needs to be dedicated to tangible and measurable outputs. Being creative for the sake of being creative *is* a productive use of time.

Creativity is within each of us. You are here, reading this book, because you prefer to express your creativity through words—you're a writer. You are meant to bring your ideas and imagination to life through the words written on a page. By engaging in your creativity, you open a window for your readers to learn from, to be entertained by, and possibly even decide to change their lives after engaging with your work.

Consider what is gained from engaging in creativity. It can offer a way to relax, to tune out the world and connect back to ourselves. It can fill us with joy and rejuvenate us. Imagine how you might move about your life with increased energy just because you engaged with your creativity more often. Painters are meant to paint. Musicians are meant to make music. Writers are meant to write.

You have an original piece of work that is ready to be expressed. While engaging with this creativity can be challenging, we have to actively choose to engage and nurture it without expectation or financial goals in mind. This requires being intentional with how we spend our time—carving out time in our busy schedules to prioritize our creativity. This may feel frivolous at times because there doesn't seem to be a point. To that, I will ask you this question: What is the point of engaging with your creativity? The answer to this question will be unique to each of us. For me, engaging in writing is a joyful expression of my ideas and a vehicle for creating a point of connection—not only with myself but also to help make sense of the environment around me. Writing is a joyful expression of who I am.

Engaging with our creativity allows the human force within us to play, come alive, heal, and dance around in what is possible. Creating from a place of freedom with no judgment is fully trusting ourselves. Nothing tampers with this self-trust more than putting financial pressure on our art. Trying to force our art to make a living for us—especially as we start to engage in the creative process—can lead to frustration and a whole lot of negative self-talk. I've seen a lot of writers and artists quit the moment they don't meet their financial goals. Instead of focusing on the power of their creativity, they replace it with beliefs such as, "I'm a terrible writer," "I guess this wasn't meant for me," "I'll never be as good as so-and-so," or "No one likes my art."

My favorite negative narrative of them all is the myth of the starving artist. Personally, I would love to see this messaging die. Look at the number of musicians making millions through their albums and stadium tours. There are artists who have sold multiple paintings for more than $5,000 each.

There are best-selling authors who have sold more than a million copies of their books. Artists are thriving when you take a moment to look around. And if you feel like being famous isn't for you, that is okay. You can still be financially lucrative from your art. But that's only if you want to be. Not all art is for public consumption.

The point is that none of this art would be born into the world for us to enjoy if these artists hadn't connected with their creative process. Our society is really good at celebrating the outcome, but it's the journey of how we got there that matters most. The creative journey is about being brave enough to engage with the process on your terms, in your time, and in a way that feels right for you. As you engage with your creative process, the right time to invite people to pay for your art will emerge. You'll know when it is the right time to charge people to engage with your art. Until then, your art, your creativity, is just for you.

That's why it's never too late to get started. Your creativity has been waiting for you to say yes. Now is the time. As a writer, you have a story to tell. That is enough to get started. Every book is written one word at a time. Over time, you'll have enough words to amount to a full-length book. It's that simple. It doesn't matter if it takes you decades or a few months. The important thing is that you start and keep going.

The creative process is unique to each of us. At times, it isn't going to look good to you or anyone else—it's a messy process. The important thing is to stop overthinking. It doesn't need to look a specific way. You're not doing anything wrong. Just allow it to unfold as best you can. The creative process is an invitation to allow for creativity to flow in the first place, rather than defining the boundaries of how it should be contained. It is an invitation to trust yourself and follow what feels right in the moment—especially when it makes little sense logically.

Instead of focusing on what the creative process *needs* to look like, it's more important that you engage with whatever it wants to become. The creative process is about carving out the time and allowing the door of creative potential to creak open. Even if the door is just wedged open, allowing for the possibility of creativity can invite an aliveness within you. Imagine if you committed to your writing today. What would be different in your life one year from now? What would be different five years from now? Will you have a published book? Will you have written and published more than one book? The thing is, if you don't start now, the truest expression of your creativity will never come to light. In five years, you may be wishing you had started five years ago. So, I ask you, dear writer: how are you willing to engage with your creativity?

While creativity might feel like a powerful force within us screaming to be expressed, it is really just our truest expression of being alive. It is this aliveness that can often scare us. It is asking us to face ourselves and our ideas in a way we've never done before. Creativity is an invitation to tap into our essence and engage with the flow of life at any given time.

To engage with your creativity, you don't need to be anything other than who you are, with a touch of willingness to allow the process to unfold without expectation.

To design this space, it is about deciding what you believe creativity to be. This is about dropping any need for productivity from creativity and allowing the messy process to unfold. You get to decide what creativity means to you and what beliefs you hold about the process and output. This process is akin to a messy kitchen after a dinner party. It looks like a tornado of dirty plates, pots, leftovers, and spilled drinks. But we know that plate-by-plate, the kitchen will get cleaned up, and it will sparkle again. The same is true as you continue to move through your creative process. One day, you'll have a piece of beauty that you'll be proud of—even if no one else ever sees it. You can create solely for yourself, or you can share your art with others. You get to decide. Writing is more than a creative practice—it's how we return to ourselves, again and again. The most important decision to make is to be brave enough to let yourself explore what the creative process looks like for you. And maybe even enjoy it.

After all, the story you've been avoiding is probably the one worth telling.

CHAPTER

3

On Doing Hard Things

The biggest obstacle to writing is often ourselves. If, like me, you've spent decades avoiding becoming a writer, I see you. I hadn't met anyone who was writing a book, so the fact that it wasn't coming to me easily deterred me. For the longest time, I thought writing a book was for the top students and extremely talented people "over there." Over there being some magical, foreign land that produced fairies and gifted writers. By the time I was twenty-something, I had a belief system rooted in phrases like "Writing is just a hobby," "You weren't good at English literature classes; there is no way you can be a writer," "You can't make money as a writer," "Becoming a teacher is the only way you can write books," "Being a 'writer' isn't a real job"...the list goes on. Do any of these sound familiar? Can you imagine all the books we would have missed out on if every author believed these things to be true?!

Writing a book is hard. Not only are there writing techniques to learn, but the creative process invites us to come up against the parts of ourselves that want to protect us and keep us safe from doing new things. To become the successful author that you desire, the journey goes beyond just the act of writing. It is about overcoming our inner obstacles. Writer's block, impostor syndrome, procrastination, and self-doubt are just a few of the experiences that derail our best intentions for writing a book.

Imagine if your favorite book wasn't written because the author got halfway through writing and decided to procrastinate and never finish because "writing is just a hobby." How disappointing! No author is immune to negative thought patterns—we're human after all. The important thing to remember is that no matter which beliefs may be cropping up, they are showing up for you to feel them, especially if they feel counterproductive to your writing goals. These beliefs are arriving at the right time to help you expand as your best creative self. There isn't an author in the past, present, or future who hasn't or won't experience these feelings. You are not alone. The feelings that crop up during the creative process are there because they need to be felt and transmuted into a new belief that can help carry us forward to where we want to go.

My relationship with writing has been filled with lots of ups and downs. From not believing I was good enough to be a writer and taking years away from a craft I loved to reconnecting with my passion for writing, becoming an editor, book coach, published author, and founding Her Narrative— my path was anything but linear. I believe that we each have a creative path that invites us to align with our soul's calling and transform into the person we need to become in this lifetime. By accepting that invitation to go deeper, we embark on an extraordinary adventure of unearthing what thoughts, beliefs, and feelings no longer serve us, to feel safe to accept what it is we really want.

Writing is an act of connecting with ourselves to become the person and author we want to be. That often means facing the parts of ourselves we might have been avoiding in mind, body, and spirit. When we step onto the path of doing something hard, we must grow into the person who not only has the capacity to craft their words on the page but is also brave enough to share their words with other people, no matter their response.

Writer's block, perfectionism, and self-doubt are all variations of pit stops an author may experience along the writing journey. The key is to work with them to prevent them from stopping you from reaching your goals. These feelings are showing up because you are brave enough to try something new.

When I began working with Martha, she was ambitious and ready to see her book on the shelves! As we kicked off our book coaching relationship, she started strong with her writing practice for the first month. During the second month, I noticed she was having to reschedule our sessions multiple times and only ended up having one call that month. The next month followed a similar pattern. When I finally connected with her, I asked her to explore that with me. It turned out that Martha was feeling like a fraud. She hadn't been writing much and felt embarrassed to tell me. She felt like she was failing both of us. Of course, I reassured her and invited her to go deeper. With Martha's permission, we worked through an exercise together and discovered that she was fighting a losing battle with resistance to writing because she had a deep fear of failure.

Once this feeling was identified, we were able to attach this fear to a belief that Martha was afraid to be seen. She was terrified of people reading the words she was writing. This is a real fear—I know I've experienced it too! Over the next two sessions, Martha and I worked to reshape her belief by leaning into this fear and allowing it to be there. In this process, she discovered that this fear was trying to protect her from other people's opinions and bad reviews of her book. Then, we allowed space for that feeling, which helped to soften its pull on her. Then, we focused on her *why* for writing her book and celebrated each writing session she showed up for. If you experience resistance along your writing journey like Martha did, know you are not alone. I invite you to lean into self-compassion and explore if there is an underlying belief that might be running the show.

To have the impact you desire from writing your book, it is critical that you don't become derailed by the doubt, fear, uncertainty, or any other less-than-desirable feeling. By taking a step back to regroup, we can learn powerful insights about ourselves, which then can propel us forward instead of causing us to stop writing altogether.

To get out of your own way and tap back into your writing goals and dreams, we need to build a toolkit for managing doubtful emotions. Just as we use writing tools for spell check and grammar, a set of tools can be built for when things feel hard. Let's address some of the most common areas writers get stuck and cultivate a mindset positioned for success.

Impostor Syndrome

Impostor syndrome is that nagging feeling that you're a fraud, that any success you've had is just a fluke, and that any minute now, someone's going to expose you for the fake that you are.

But here's the truth: impostor syndrome is a liar. You are not a fraud. You are talented, you are capable, and you deserve to be here. When impostor syndrome shows up, take a step back and ask yourself: Do you always feel like a fraud, or is it just some of the time? For most of us, impostor syndrome shows up when we are in a period of growth. We are stepping outside of our comfort zones and are stretching ourselves in a new area. It's a signal that we're expanding. As a writer, it is not uncommon to feel this as you step into the arena and start putting words on the page. You might start comparing yourself to authors who are ten steps further down the road than you are. At the beginning of our journey, it can be easy to picture the finish line and wonder why we aren't there yet.

Impostor syndrome can also be an indicator that you're headed in the right direction. That means you're only an impostor for as long as you are unwilling to learn. The more you keep learning, the more knowledge you have and the more you are expanding. If you choose to stop learning, well, I'm not here to call anyone names.

It's only if you choose to no longer write the book that impostor syndrome wins. Impostor syndrome is only a label for those who are unwilling to take the next step. You're not an impostor; you're a writer creating your legacy. You're not a fast food meal; you're a Michelin-starred eight-course meal that deserves to be savored. That isn't done overnight. You are exactly where you need to be, but this does require a commitment to keep moving forward.

Here are two suggestions to help you work with impostor syndrome when it arises:

Cultivate Self-Compassion

We are often our harshest critic. Instead of beating yourself up every time you make a mistake (because let's face it, we all make mistakes), try meeting yourself with ten percent more kindness. If it is helpful, you can also think about your best friend or your pet—how would they treat you in this moment? Self-compassion is a muscle that can take time to develop if self-grace hasn't been plentiful in the past. It can be easy to berate ourselves for not making the progress we want with our writing. (I've been there!)

The next time you start to notice negative self-talk arise, try this: close your eyes, take a deep breath, and repeat after me: "I am human. I am making progress, and that is enough." Feels better already, doesn't it?

Embrace Your Wins

If impostor syndrome could talk, it might say something like, "You haven't done anything significant yet." That's simply not true. When this feels true, take a moment to review what you have achieved. I'm talking about celebrating every victory, no matter how small. Did you think about writing today? Celebrate. Did you sit down and write? Celebrate. Finish a chapter? Celebrate. Receive a positive book review? Celebrate. Write a killer sentence? You guessed it—celebrate!

Every celebration doesn't require a Formula One podium-level champagne spray—unless you want it to. It can be as simple as taking a walk in the sunshine or making a cup of tea. It's the act of acknowledgement that fuels your continued progress. The pause to celebrate can also silence that voice that tells you that you haven't done enough.

Go ahead, celebrate your wins like the rock star writer you are!

Impostor syndrome may be an unwelcome guest on your writing journey, but it doesn't have to be in the driver's seat. With a little self-awareness and a frequent dash of self-compassion, you can begin to work with this feeling and keep writing. Provide yourself with the evidence that you are not an alien impostor. You are simply a person on a writing journey, taking it one step at a time, *just like every author before you.*

Self-Doubt

If there were an annoying sibling to impostor syndrome, it would be self-doubt. Self-doubt can sneak in and cause you to second-guess every word you write. It can create a spiral of questions around what you are not capable of. But here's the thing: self-doubt is fear in disguise. It might be a fear of failure, a fear of not being good enough, a fear of putting yourself out there, or a fear of rejection. Fear and self-doubt are masks for many of the beliefs discussed earlier around what it means to be a broke artist and question if your writing will ever be good enough. These statements are what we call a limiting belief.

A limiting belief is a false idea that we believe to be true about ourselves. These stem from our family's belief systems, society, and life experience. When these beliefs go unchecked, they can hold us back from doing what it is we really want to do. They act as invisible force fields that can hold us back. The good news? These limiting beliefs can be molded and reworked to help us move forward in the way we desire.

The next time self-doubt or fear comes knocking, try this:

1. Acknowledge it.
2. Thank this belief for its input.
3. Then, respectfully reframe it into a statement that helps you focus on what you want. For example, if self-doubt is producing the belief that you are a terrible writer, a reframe might be, "Every time I write, I become better and better at my craft."

The goal here is not to swing into toxic positivity but rather to encourage our brains to focus on expanding into what is possible instead of getting tripped up on the negative belief cycles written in the past.

One of my favorite quotes from the book *The War of Art* by Steven Pressfield says, "Self-doubt can be an ally. This is because it serves as an indicator of aspiration. It reflects love, love of something we dream of doing, and desire, desire to do it."[11]

When our fears and doubts are activated, it is a signal that we're shaking up the status quo. We're looking into the distance, wondering what could be different. That's exciting, albeit a little scary. As you embark on a writing journey, you are doing something new. You are doing something unknown, and your brain just wants to know you'll be safe along the way. That is why learning to work with these emotions can be the most important thing we do, aside from learning the craft of writing. When we suppress or dismiss these emotions, that is when we become at war with ourselves. We become our biggest obstacle, and that is when we throw in the towel, saying things like, "Never mind. I tried; I'm not meant to be an author." To that, I say: Nope. Not on my watch. You have a powerful story to write, and the world needs it. As you expand into this new version of yourself, please have grace. Allow space for what needs to come up and go at your own pace. Getting derailed is not an option.

Writer's Block

Every writer experiences the frustration of writer's block at some point in their creative journey. The inability to put words on the page or the absence of the next great idea can be disheartening.

When the dreaded writer's block rears its ugly head, frustration and disappointment often follow suit. Whether you've hit a sudden roadblock in your writing progress or are eagerly awaiting the arrival of the next best-selling idea, know that no writer is immune to this creative obstacle.

Instead of harshly pushing through, I encourage you to consider shifting away from your logical brain and tapping into your heart and inner wisdom. To do this, I recommend moving your body in ways that are available to you, such as dancing, yoga, or a walk. It might feel counterintuitive to step away from your computer, but by allowing this space, you can tap into your inner wisdom and give your brain a moment to stop overthinking and continually search for the answers.

When writer's block emerges, try these tips:

Change Your Environment

A change of environment can do wonders for our brains. When we can step away from our routines and explore opportunities to step out of our writing environments, we get to observe life. After all, the best stories often emerge from life itself. A change of scenery can provide the fresh perspective needed to break through creative barriers.

A new environment can be a powerful catalyst, providing the clarity needed to overcome creative barriers. Personally, I find solace in stepping away from my computer and taking a walk. A simple stroll around town has miraculously resolved many plot holes.

Become an Observer of Life

Another effective strategy for writer's block involves engaging with the world outside your writing space. Meeting friends for dinner or simply eavesdropping on conversations in public spaces can provide a wealth of inspiration (in a non-stalkery way, of course!). Overhearing snippets of dialogue, witnessing unique interactions, or absorbing the atmosphere of a new setting can infuse your work with a dose of authenticity and creativity. Inspiration often strikes when we least expect it, and embracing the unpredictable nature of these moments can be a game-changer.

Reflect on Thoughts and Beliefs

Writer's block can stem from self-doubt, fear of failure, perfectionism, or even burnout. Identify and explore any less-than-desirable thoughts or beliefs that arise when experiencing writer's block. Often, writer's block can be a cloak for when we are being overly critical of ourselves. If this appears to be the case, take a moment to write down any negative thoughts without judgment or analysis. Say thank you to these thoughts and allow them to exist neutrally. Then, set them aside as you return to your day.

Recognizing the underlying factors contributing to writer's block is crucial for developing targeted strategies to overcome it. Journaling about these feelings and exploring their origins can be a therapeutic way to untangle the web of emotions that often accompanies creative stagnation.

Embracing the ebb and flow of the creative process is essential for every writer facing the challenge of writer's block. By incorporating mindful yet powerful techniques, like changing your environment and reflecting on your thoughts and beliefs, you can navigate through the complex terrain of creative barriers with grace. Trust in your process and remember that the words will flow when the time is right.

Procrastination

At the root of procrastination is often perfectionism. It's an unrealistic expectation of ourselves, this inability to accept anything less than perfect. We all know that perfection is an impossible feat, which can cause a tailspin if we focus on it for too long. Writing is meant to be an unknown and untidy process. No writer has ever sat down and written a perfect book as their first draft.

If you find yourself procrastinating, ask yourself what lies behind that feeling. If you need rest, then rest. If you are falling into the trap of perfectionism, then take a breath, and remember that you are in the middle of an unfolding writing process. The point is not to be perfect, but to keep showing up, to keep making progress.

Resistance can show up and cause us to become a kicking and screaming toddler who doesn't want to write. The burning desire to just be done writing the book can be a fiery one. If you find yourself should-ing yourself, meaning you are shaming yourself into writing because you think that is what you should be doing, pause. Ask yourself what it is that you need. Sometimes forcing ourselves to write is the worst thing we can do. Just because you have twenty extra minutes doesn't mean you need to fill that time. Allow yourself to rest. The ideas and writing will flow when you feel less resistance to writing.

If what you're feeling isn't exhaustion, but rather just annoyance with the process of writing or feeling like you're not in the creative flow—write. By engaging with the process of writing, you can soften the resistance. You show yourself that showing up is what matters, and word by word, your book will get written. When we choose to do hard things—like become a writer—it serves us well to learn and understand the difference between resistance and needing rest.

Grief in the Writing Process

Grief is not synonymous with writing. This is a feeling state I don't see the writing world often talking about. Grief can show up in many different ways throughout the writing process. For the authors that I've worked with, it has come up in the following ways:

- Grief from letting go of what they thought the book would be and allowing it to become what it needs to be.
- Grief from revisiting painful time periods in their lives.
- Grief from letting go of some of the words they wrote while editing.

Writing and publishing books conveys a sense of excitement, but grief can be a part of the writing process for many authors. This is often a surprise for authors. As you are writing, if you find yourself experiencing grief for any reason, from reliving past painful experiences to letting go of what you thought your writing process might be to grieving having to edit down and cut pieces of your book, it is all okay. Allow grief to be a part of your writing journey as it needs to be. It can be easy to want to push away grief, but when we can lean into it, it can be a powerful source that can fuel our creativity.

I was working with an author who was writing a fiction book based on a tragic event that happened to their family years prior, which resulted in the loss of a family member. This was a very personal story, but it also touched on the universal themes of love, loss, and managing grief. As the editor and book coach, I had to walk a fine line and take my lead from the author to ensure I wasn't pushing them to relive a painful period while also holding space to ensure the story would connect with readers. During the editing process, this author was processing multiple types of grief. One was the literal death of this family member. The second was mourning the change in their writing style. They were not new to writing, but their prior experience had been writing nonfiction. The shift to fiction was asking them to reshape their writing voice, tone, and technique, which resulted in its own sense of grief.

When grief arises, take time to pause. Allow whatever is coming up to come up. If you need to step away from your writing for a while, that is okay too. Remember in the previous chapter where the word intention, as defined by the medical field, means "the healing process of a wound." Grief is a part of the healing process. If your writing invites you to revisit painful periods in your life, remember you are sharing this not to rehash how you gained a wound, but to share the lessons learned from that experience. Focusing and becoming clear on the lesson in the experience and the importance of sharing it can allow a healthy distance without requiring you to relive the experience. No matter if or when grief shows up for you in the writing process, be gentle with yourself.

To do hard things, we have to become obsessed with the process. Talent and interest don't mean writing will come easily. This means embracing all aspects of the process—the good, the bad, and the in between. This means allowing yourself the space to grieve and lean into all the feeling states as they arise. As you are evolving in your writing and creative process, you are meeting new parts of yourself, addressing outdated beliefs, and shedding parts that are no longer needed in this next stage of your evolution. As you continue down the path of your writing journey and these feeling states arise, bookmark these pages for the support you need in those moments. It's amazing how, when we can sit with our resistance or undesired feelings, they can soften their hold. After all, evolution hurts the most right before the breakthrough moments.

You've chosen a mission to write a book, which is no easy task. The truth is, you may lose your spark along the way. You may become disinterested in writing. You may have a ton of ideas for books and never commit to one—maybe starting another book is a better idea! This is all resistance to the growth.

Many individuals who set out to write a book will stop well before they finish a first draft. This is similar to the fizzling out of New Year's resolutions by February. It can be easy to start out with clear intentions, but when we hit a wall of expansion, it's easy to shrink back and say, "Never mind." The good news is that by reading this book, you're gaining the knowledge and tools for managing self-doubt and the beliefs that will come up along the writing journey. By reading this far, success is already inevitable for you.

There will always be more evidence for your fears than your dreams. It's all about how you reconcile the two while honoring yourself so that you are no longer the biggest obstacle to your success. As a wise business coach once told me, "You can only grow your business as much as you're willing to grow yourself." I have found this advice to be true not only for being an entrepreneur but for being a writer. To reach our goals, we have to be willing to meet parts of ourselves that create resistance to protect us from doing something new, so that we can expand as a person. What makes this even more tricky is that growth isn't linear. It's more like a spiral staircase that moves us up in the right direction, but we often have to loop back around past the things we thought we had outgrown. I invite you to hold space for your evolution.

This starts with being willing to reevaluate unconscious beliefs that have been driving the show. Personally, I had to reshape my identity so that I could show up as the person who could welcome a new era of being and lead others to do the same. It means being brave enough to believe in your vision before anyone else does. Every day will be different, but as you show up consistently, you'll find that writing can become a healing outlet. Perhaps you are writing about past experiences that bring up a lot of emotion. Maybe you find grief has found its way into your writing process. Perhaps self-doubt has crept back in. Breathe. Writing is your sacred practice if you choose for it to be. It transcends the act of writing a book; it can be therapeutic.

That doesn't mean that every diary entry you've ever written needs to be in your book, but if journaling or writing just to explore emotions or your creativity outside of what you are working on in your book shows up—allow it. Get curious. Tune into your emotions to feel what it is they are inviting you to explore, release, or nurture. Honor your feelings and experiences as they arise, but don't get stuck in one place. When the time is right, keep moving forward.

Think of a seed breaking through the cold ground in early spring. It's freezing, uncomfortable, and unclear what is going to happen next. Just like a plant doesn't bloom all at once, meet yourself at the growth stage you are at. What do you need? Is it to rest? Is it to learn? Is it to read and get inspired? Is it to reduce the total time you write per week? Is it to allow the manuscript to rest for a while? Dig into what you need and then do that.

Writing can be both a creative and a spiritual act. And while the focus of this chapter was on the less desirable feeling states that might arise along the writing journey, it is equally important to recognize that the writing journey can also be filled with joy, happiness, fulfillment, delight, excitement, contentment, and pure ecstasy. Writing is more than just a means for creating a piece of published work. If you are open, a lot of beauty can unfold.

CHAPTER

4

The Light of Your Words

Your story is the light someone else needs to find their way. It is easy to underestimate the power of your words. You are not writing a "silly little book just for fun." You're exploring ideas, creating worlds, and presenting methods—all of which can move someone in their heart, mind, and life. It just takes one sentence that resonates with a reader, shifting their soul or moving them into action. Your words can pave the path they need to keep going. Think of your favorite authors. If they were derailed from the limited beliefs and experiences we explored in the previous chapter, we would have missed out on so many powerful and amazing stories. By sharing your story, you're inviting readers deeper into the human experience.

Take, for instance, a self-development book. If you are the author, your book may be the catalyst that inspires a reader to finally go after their biggest dreams. Or maybe a reader sees themselves in your romance protagonist and realizes they also need to embrace love and no longer hide from it. Who knows, maybe your book inspires them to say "Yes" to a first date! You never know. The ideas and concepts presented in your book have the ability to plant a seed in the reader's mind. That seed could blossom into positive change.

Books are a way for humans to experience life through the eyes of another. When universal themes such as love, grief, happiness, fear, and sadness come through on the page, the reader can see themselves in these experiences. This has the potential to expand the perspective of the reader to explore what could be different in their own lives. It can help them learn how others respond and react to life events. On a subconscious level, their brains might even begin to log how they can respond to a similar event in real life. In *Wired for Story*, Lisa Cron writes, "Stories allow us to simulate intense experiences without having to actually live through them. Stories allow us to experience the world before we actually have to experience it."[12] The more we can explore human experiences through books, the more we can relate to others on a deeper level because we have lived a similar experience through reading. This connection is the birthplace of understanding and empathy. Through the art of writing, we get to explore what it means to be in full human expression. If we allow it, writing is a personal and transformative ritual. To write is to heal. It is the act of caring for those who read our words.

The most powerful words written are when the reader feels seen in your story—maybe for the very first time. The light of your words can connect readers to themselves in ways they haven't been able to before. Perhaps they have always felt different, and your book welcomes them into a whole new community of people where that difference is the norm. There is a power in being witnessed. Readers will care about your book because we all want to be seen. Let your story allow others to see themselves with their highest potential.

The power of your experiences, ideas, and insights captured in a book can pave a way forward for your reader. Your words hold deep meaning. One sentence can help a reader reframe how they see a situation in their life. Each reader will take away what they need to in that moment from your book. But here is the catch: it's not your job to determine which line will be the light. It's your responsibility to write the words. Your story is like a rain drop landing in a lake; it can cause a ripple effect well beyond what you could imagine—if you allow it.

I've had the pleasure of working with a number of authors who are writing on topics that aren't considered mainstream. From spirituality books exploring what it means to be a Starseed to business books that remind us that it's not just about strategy, it is about embodying our minds and souls, to a utopian novel that dismantles our capitalist society and rebuilds a more equitable and beautiful world. No matter the genre, all these authors' books had the power to expand and transform what a reader thought was possible for themselves and the world around them. These authors have written books that don't always fit into the mainstream narrative, yet they have received immense amounts of positive feedback on their books. Readers have told them how much their books inspired them and given them permission to rethink how they live, work, and carve out time for their spirituality. That is one of the coolest parts of my job as an editor: I get to read these books before anyone else, and even in the development stage, the writing will tap into my heart, and I feel seen in new ways with every project I work on.

That is the power and impact that your words hold. That impact is established by defining *why* you are writing your book.

The Why Behind Your Book

Your why is the compass that guides your entire book. It's a compass that helps provide direction for where you need to go next and where you want to end up. Without it, you can stray, get lost at sea, and wonder why you even set out on this voyage in the first place. Earlier, I asked what your intent was for writing a book. This tends to be a personal endeavor or a soul calling. Defining your why for writing a book is a more focused mission statement that can help guide you along the writing process.

Writing a book is a process. There will be times when it feels too hard to continue, and you potentially want to scrap the whole thing and toss it out the window. That is where having a clear why to anchor back into comes into play. It reminds you of why you got started in the first place. It's during those tough days that reconnecting with your why will help fuel you forward.

More importantly, your why for writing your book is connecting with your personal emotional resonance to your story. Just as your story connects with readers through emotion, your why for writing your book is the bridge between your intent and the actions of writing. Having a clear why evokes your emotional engagement, which drives motivation.[13]

One author I worked with, Rebecca, was a highly motivated and highly creative entrepreneur who helped women business owners generate more income within their businesses. Rebecca was setting out to write her first book after having published a lot of content through her courses, blog, and TEDx talk. We started working together after she had written most of her book, but she felt stuck on how to get from the middle of her book to a completed manuscript. Through the book coaching process, I was able to ask her powerful questions that helped her refine why she was writing this book, who it was for, and how her book would be impactful for readers. During these moments of feeling stuck, when she was able to tap back into the emotions of her why for writing her book, her motivation would ignite and she was able to revisit her outline, move a few pieces around, delete a few sections, and continue to move toward a first draft of her book—all within four months. Rebeca's story illustrates the importance of not only tapping into the emotions of why we're going after what we are, but also how having a clear destination can be a powerful motivator.

To help you get clear on your why, ask yourself: Why do you feel compelled to write this specific book? What deeper personal meaning or emotional truth is driving you to write this book?

There is no right or wrong answer here. It could be a combination of things—anything from having a calling to write the book, to wanting this book to position you as a thought leader in your industry, to leaving a legacy, or personal healing and transformation. You get to decide. The important piece here is that you're clear on why you are writing the book, so that when it gets hard, you have a personal guidance system to tap back into to keep you motivated toward the end goal.

A few examples of why statements from authors I've worked with include:

- "I'm writing this book because I want others to feel seen and understood, the way books made me feel during the hardest parts of my life."
- "This story has lived inside me for years, and writing it is my way of honoring my voice—and proving to myself that my story matters."

- "I want to create a legacy for my children, showing them that it's never too late to pursue a dream or share your truth."

- "I'm writing this because the lessons I've learned could help someone else find hope, strength, or a new path forward."

- "Telling this story is a way of healing my own past—and offering healing to anyone who might recognize themselves in these pages."

Once you are clear on your why, write it down. I also invite you to reference it often. Bonus: Look at it before you sit down to write.

As you write, you will likely be pulling from personal experiences. This can be very cathartic in processing the past and allowing yourself to reflect on what you have learned. When we reflect on the experiences in our lives, it can be easy to downplay the significance they hold. No matter if you are writing fiction or nonfiction, there is always an element of our lives being interwoven into our stories. It is the human experience and human emotions that connect the author and the reader through the page. We're not getting out of here without some wounds. But to not share the battles you've fought to only present a polished, happy ending not only does you a disservice, but it also does a disservice to your audience. Happy endings promote the idea of instant gratification. In a way, it leads to more suffering if an audience doesn't understand the full journey.

I've always struggled with this in the business world. I've listened to leaders across many industries speak at live events or on podcasts, and they belittle how hard things in the middle were. They belittle challenges by saying they just made a phone call, or someone magically showed up and introduced them to the resource they had been seeking. That's not to say those things aren't happening, but I don't believe for one minute there wasn't also fear, confusion, self-questioning, and concern about their next move.

Most honest and successful people will tell you there were a lot of challenges and failures before they reached a level of being renowned, wealthy, or famous. Most overnight successes are at least ten years in the making. When you are writing, don't downplay your experiences; lean into them. There are nuggets of insight that can be a light for others lost in the dark tunnel of the human experience.

Your words have the ability to meet readers right where they are and provide them with what they need at that moment in time. Perhaps the whole purpose of your story is to help someone feel a little less alone. That is why your story is needed. Your words shine bright—let them through! I truly believe storytelling is not only a powerful tool for self-expression and empowerment but also a way to challenge perceptions, build empathy, and foster community.

Your voice matters. Your story matters. By writing, you are unapologetically sharing it with the world, knowing that it will have an impact. This is the power of being an intentional writer on a mindful journey to writing a book.

Through the process of getting clear on the why behind writing your book, you not only create a lighthouse guiding you toward the finish line, but you open a container and space to allow your words to land on the page in a way that will light the path for others.

CHAPTER

5

Uncovering the Heart of Your Story

The heart of your story expands beyond your foundational why—it holds a purpose for readers. When a reader has a clear understanding of why *they* are reading your book, they commit to following your every word until the final page.

Your why for writing your book is also important to understand the purpose of your story. You have your reasons for writing the book, and the reader has their reasons for choosing to read your book. Your why is personal, whereas the purpose of your book is what motivates your reader to read it. A clear purpose statement for your book makes a promise to your readers about what they will experience by investing their money, time, and energy into reading your book.

In other words, getting to the heart of your story can pull at the heartstrings of readers. Books that have a clear purpose are the ones that resonate the most with readers and provide them with a compelling reason for reading your book.

To uncover the heart of your story, we need to explore two areas: the theme(s) of your book and the reason for your book's existence. These elements will come together in what I call your Book Concept Statement. Defining your Book Concept Statement not only tells the readers exactly what your book is about, but it will help you frame what you write in your book.

When you know the theme—or themes—of your book, it becomes the beating heart that keeps your story moving. When the theme is clear, it becomes a filter to help you decide which stories or scenes help to illustrate that theme. It can also help to guide you to see if you've strayed from your original intent for the book.

The theme of your book doesn't have to be a formal statement. Book themes often explore universal human experiences such as grief, growth, sadness, loneliness, happiness, success, love, ambition, etc. For example, if you are a relationship coach writing a book to help couples reconnect, you might have a book theme centered around the experience of love conquering fear. If you are writing a historical fiction novel taking place during wartime, you might be exploring the theme of how war can destroy innocence and challenge relationships. While your story on the surface is about survival during war times, the theme holds a deeper meaning around the cost of war on an individual's relationships.

I've worked with several authors writing memoirs, and throughout their writing process, they wrote diary entries that chronologically told their life story, unsure of how each entry added value to the larger story. That is where their book's theme and purpose statement came in handy. By becoming clear on these two elements, your writing will become focused on the core message at hand. In other words, when the moral of your story is clear, you will have a stronger understanding of the purpose behind each chapter in your book and how it all serves the larger story arc of your book.

To help you get clear on the intended impact your book will have, spend some time answering the following questions:

- What is the core idea or theme(s) of my book?
- If I had to explain what my book was about in one sentence, what would it be?
- How do I want readers to feel after reading my book? (They might feel inspired, educated, entertained, moved by emotion, or something else.)
- If you are writing nonfiction: What problem, question, or challenge does my book address?
- How does my unique voice, background, or knowledge inform my writing?

By taking the time to answer these questions, you are taking the time to craft a well-defined purpose to keep your writing focused and meaningful. Once you feel these answers are complete, let's use this information to create your Book Concept Statement. Just like your why for writing the book will be a personal anchor as you write, your Book Concept Statement will be a guiding light for your book and the content you plan to write.

Creating Your Book Concept Statement

With an idea behind your book's theme(s) and desired impact, let's take it a step further by defining your Book Concept Statement. Think of this as a vision statement ensuring every chapter, scene, or section aligns with the message you want to convey. Having a clear concept statement behind your book also helps to meet readers' expectations because they gain a clear understanding of what your book is about, even if you don't share this statement with them. Your Book Concept Statement helps to set the tone for your writing and for what the reader can expect to gain from reading your book.

Depending on the genre, a Book Concept Statement will focus on either the protagonist's journey, as is the case with fiction, or on the reader as the main character, as is the case with nonfiction. For example, if you are writing a personal development book about how rest can fuel progress, you—as the author—will be talking directly to the reader, making them the main character. You will be helping them go from a state of depletion to a restful state by the time they finish reading. The goal of a Book Concept Statement is to help you get clear on who your book is for, why it matters to them, and what they will take away from reading your book. Let's explore a few frameworks for both nonfiction and fiction to help you sculpt your Book Concept Statement.

Nonfiction Book Concept Statement Template

For nonfiction books that are focused on personal development or how-tos, the following Book Concept Statement template helps to define the types of readers who will be interested in your book's topic, address the challenges they are facing, and provide a solution so that they can move forward in an area of their life:

This book helps **[audience/readers]** understand **[problem, topic, or challenge]** by providing **[method, strategy, or insight]**, so they can **[desired outcome or transformation]**.

As mentioned above, it can be helpful to position your reader as the main character to identify the journey you are going to take them on and what their transformation will be by the time they finish reading your book. At the beginning of your book, the reader is likely feeling stuck or needing a resource to move forward with a goal, and they get the sense that your book will be the solution they are seeking. Your book offers a transformation. By getting clear on where they are at the beginning of your book (e.g., stuck, unsure, confused), you can then establish who they will become by the end of your book (e.g., confident, clear, inspired). What is the journey you are taking the reader on, and how will they benefit? Here is an example of a Book Concept Statement for a personal development book:

"This book teaches women how to overcome self-doubt and embrace their personal power through practical, science-backed strategies for building confidence and resilience."

This example defines the audience as "women" who are facing a "challenge around self-doubt," and this book offers a solution of "practical, science-backed strategies" to help these readers "build confidence and resilience," which is the transformation.

If you are writing creative nonfiction, such as a memoir that follows the story of your life, you can still consider how the reader may be transformed from reading your story or what they will feel as a result of reading your book.

Fiction Book Concept Statement Template

To write a Book Concept Statement for fiction, position the main character as the focus. After all, the story is about their journey. It is through understanding and relating to the main character that readers are transported into another world and have a positive reading experience.

In a **[setting/genre]**, a **[main character description]** must **[primary goal or action]** in order to **[stakes or consequence]**, but faces **[main conflict/obstacle]** along the way.

The fiction Book Concept Statement sets the stage by being clear about where this book takes place or which genre it falls under. A genre is defined by the type of fiction book, for example, fantasy, romance, contemporary, women's fiction, mystery, thriller, historical, etc.

The next portion of this Book Concept Statement provides a description that defines the main character. The goal here is for someone to quickly get a sense of who this person is through a description of their physical features, such as gender, an eye patch, a limp, or an adjective such as shy, confident, or slinky, so that we can instantly picture this person. Next, include a description of what it is they want. This is the key to all fiction books—the protagonist needs to want something. That is the fuel that drives your story. This provides the reader with context for why this story is taking place. Next, there needs to be an element of the consequences that could play out if they don't get what they want. What will that loss mean for their life?

The last portion of the concept statement for fiction is to highlight the main conflict that will take place in the story based on the character going for what they want. What or who is going to get in the way of them going after their desires? Another way to think about this is, what is at stake for your character? What is at risk if they don't accomplish what it is they want to do?

An example of a Book Concept Statement for a contemporary fiction book might look like this:

> "After a tragic accident, a woman rediscovers her identity and learns to love again by rebuilding her life in a small coastal town where secrets from her past resurface."

This concept statement starts with the main conflict, which is labeled "a tragic accident." The main character, a "woman," must "rediscover her identity," which is what's at stake, or "rebuild[ing] her life" as she wants, where there are consequences of finding out "secrets from her past."

The accident is what kicks off the story, with the unfolding of what the response to this incident will be, "rebuilding her life." We know from this statement that we will be following this woman's journey to rebuild her life in a small coastal town.

Memoir Book Concept Statement Template

Memoir is unique in that it's a genre that is categorized as nonfiction but benefits from being written as a novel. If you are writing a memoir, then you, the author, are the main character telling the audience about a period of time in your life.

This memoir shows **[audience]** what it's like to **[core experience or challenge]**, revealing how **[main struggle or theme]** can lead to **[transformation or insight]**, so they can **[emotional outcome or sense of connection]**.

The memoir Book Concept Statement sets the stage for why the reader will be drawn into your story and what they will feel as a result of reading your book.

An example of a Book Concept Statement for a memoir book might look like this:

"This memoir shows readers what it's like to grow up in a wildly unconventional and often neglectful family, revealing how surviving chaos and instability can lead to fierce independence and self-reliance, so they can better understand the resilience of the human spirit and the complexity of family bonds."

This concept statement not only positions you, the author, as the main character but tells the reader exactly what themes come through in your story.

No matter if you are writing fiction or nonfiction, creating a Book Concept Statement provides a way for you to get crystal clear on what the reader's experience will be. As you begin writing your book, you can revisit this statement often to see if you're still on track to deliver the intended purpose of your book. Since the writing process can also be a discovery process, your purpose statement might evolve as you continue to write. If that is the case, you're not doing anything wrong. Come back to your Book Concept Statement to see if anything needs to be adjusted to match the new direction of your story. Just because your story evolves as you write doesn't mean you have to make it fit into your Book Concept Statement.

Being flexible during the writing process allows you to ebb and flow with what insight emerges during the act of writing that will make your story the most impactful. The key to using the Book Concept Statement is to provide a North Star that will keep your writing focused so that it delivers your intended experience for the reader.

When I set out to write this book, I used this process to craft my own Book Concept Statement, which has helped me to stay focused on the key topics presented, avoid unnecessary fluffy detours, and bring each chapter back to the heart of my story. I set out to write this book because I got tired of the how-to-write-a-book content mainly focusing on only the technical craft pieces while neglecting to take an intentional and holistic approach to the creative process that nurtures the author, the reader, and the content while acknowledging just how hard the writing journey can really be. I found a lot of the writing advice out there was built on hustle culture, and that didn't work for me. As someone who works primarily with women and underrepresented voices, and who also has a deep sense of mindfulness, I believe we are dynamic individuals with stories that we want others to learn from, grow from, consider a new perspective from, or be inspired by. I created this book to sit at the intersection of the craft of writing and mindset pieces that help nurture you into the author you've always dreamed of becoming. At the very least, as authors, we want readers to enjoy reading our book as much as we enjoyed writing it. This book was designed for you—the mindful writer—who is ready to express your truest soul's expression through intentional writing practices that leave your mark on the world in a way that nurtures you.

By using the Book Concept Statement, I ensured I was clear on the experience I wanted to provide for you. Similarly, my novels fit under the women's fiction genre—no surprise there! I love writing about female protagonists who reconnect to their core essence and then go for what they want. This is a central theme that comes through in my writing (and my work). I believe in the power of having diverse perspectives on the bookshelves, no matter the genre. The Book Concept Statement allows me to take these themes and highlight them further to help direct my focus to produce books that—you, the readers—love.

By taking the time to become clear on your why for writing a book, your book's theme, and a defined concept statement, you now hold the keys to craft a story with intention. You now have a friendly anchor to help you remain tethered to your intent and purpose that will help guide your story forward without derailing you.

I recommend keeping your why statement, book theme, and concept statement visible during your writing sessions. Personally, I have these statements written on bright pink Post-it notes on my desk. These vibrant, eye-catching notes are a way for me to reconnect both to my why and the book's purpose as I continue to write and develop this book. Keeping my eye on the big picture helps me when I get stuck or become unsure of what I need to write next. When I reconnect with these statements, I am able to remind myself of my intent and connect to what you—the reader— need to know next. This clarity helps me shape this book in a way that I know will help you write the book of your dreams.

A few years ago, I was working with a very successful executive leader who works across continents, making the world spin while we all go about our daily lives. She had decided to take a sabbatical, and one of her goals for this period of time was to write a book to help shape the next generation of business leaders. We collaborated during the first round of edits for her book. During my first read-through, it became clear that her reason for writing the book had become lost during the writing process. While she had compelling points backed by data, the reason for a reader to keep reading and why it was relevant to them was not evident.

When we met to discuss next steps in her editing process, I encouraged her to take a step away from the details of the words on the page and revisit her why for writing the book and why readers should care. While her intent for writing the book was to help inform and shape the future of leadership within the corporate world, that purpose was also a lofty goal that took her on many detours throughout the book that didn't connect to her original intention. I provided her with some of the questions and framework I've shared with you here to gain clarity. She came back to me with the following why statement:

"To ensure my career and personal successes not only leave my legacy but also help to inspire other women to embrace their strengths and go for what they want."

She also came back with this Book Concept Statement:

"To help the next generation of female leaders connect heart and mind to move businesses forward."

With a newfound sense of purpose, we were able to map the reader's journey based on this why working as our anchor or filter to ensure that each chapter built upon the previous to lead readers to this destination. Did this mean reshaping a large portion of her book? Yes. But did she elevate her reader experience and create more impact by getting clear on not only why she was writing it, but why she was writing it for a specific audience? Heck yes!

By taking the time to become clear on the heart of your story, the writing process will unfold with greater ease and flow. The Book Concept Statement provides a sense of direction, acting as a guiding light or a compass, helping you to navigate the writing process. This guiding light will not only help you make progress when writing but will be an anchor you can come back to when self-doubt, procrastination, or writer's block emerge. Your why and Book Concept Statement are tools to help you tap back into the essence of your book at any stage of the writing journey. If you haven't already, I invite you to play around with creating your Book Concept Statement and displaying it in a place you can reference often.

CHAPTER

6

Outlining with Intention

A good outline isn't a cage—it's a guide to keep you on track. In the writing world, there is much discussion around being a pantser—someone who writes by the seat of their pants—or being a plotter—someone who plans out every detail before writing.

Both pantsing and plotting can be effective ways to approach writing a book. And, if you're anything like me, you might fall somewhere in between these two camps. I tend to be a lady with a plan, but I also like the organic unfolding of what could happen along the way.

While an outline may feel like a cage to someone who craves creative expression, it can provide the backbone to your success in completing your book. It's a guide that helps to map out your next step. After all, creativity does thrive when it has a clear direction.

The process of writing a book is similar to building a house. The foundation consists of your why, your themes, and your Book Concept Statement. Once that is established, it is time to frame the walls, which is equivalent to your outline. Each chapter is a room in your house—you need to be clear about where each room will be and what furnishings will reside in each room.

A clear outline is one of the most powerful tools in the writing process. Outlining gives your intention for writing a book the structure to frame your ideas. This helps you see the big picture while guiding you toward each scene or section with purpose.

That's not to say that some of your story won't unfold as you are writing—best laid plans and all that. That is perfectly okay. The goal here is to establish an outline that gives you confidence to dive into the writing process with intention and direction.

The outline process is all about creating an intentional space that will hold your ideas and help them take shape in a way that will be most impactful and digestible for the reader. What you outline now doesn't have to be the exact path you take—heck, this book started with a very clear outline only for me to move more than half the chapters around! An outline is a starting point that helps you frame the key milestones and events along your storytelling journey. There will be places where you can pause, reevaluate, and redirect as needed. The goal with your outline is to have a sturdy jumping-off place to direct your writing.

If you prefer to write from the seat of your pants, I get it. I was that way too. In fact, I'm still like that most of the time. However, I have learned to start with an outline so that I can see the key plot points and story beats to help me know what I am working toward in each section of my book. It's like putting a road trip destination in the GPS knowing that you're going to stop at fruit stands, viewpoints, and coffee shops along the way. The point is, it's okay to stop along your route; you just want to avoid unnecessary detours or getting stuck, never making it to your final destination.

For many authors, planning out every detail ahead of writing is helpful. For me, having every detail plotted out ahead of time distracts me from getting words on the page. The invitation here is to explore what you need from the outlining process to feel like you have enough direction to sit down and write.

For myself and Lauri, an author I collaborated with, we both had hit a wall around the 20,000-word mark when writing our first books. This is not an uncommon experience for writers during their first book. Approaching the "messy middle" often feels confusing because you've seen a lot of your story's plot unfold, and while there is more to share, you have no idea how you're going to write approximately 80,000 words to reach the end of your book. That is where outlining can be a powerful tool.

When I worked with Lauri to write an outline for her book, we used the three-act structure. This provided her with a framework to help guide her, while also providing her the space to allow her creativity and imagination to flow in between the key moments she was writing toward. By creating an outline, Lauri was not only able to reengage with her first book, but she was also able to save time and write without feeling frustrated. An outline is not a lifelong marriage agreement; it's a guideline helping to organize your thoughts while allowing the space for creative inspiration.

Whether you are writing fiction or nonfiction, an outline can keep your work focused, improve pacing, and ensure every part of your book serves a purpose. To help you do just that, this chapter is divided into two separate sections to help both fiction and nonfiction writers take an intentional approach to the outlining process. There is much to gain from both approaches, so don't feel limited to just reading the section that pertains to your genre.

Nonfiction Book Outlining

In this section, we'll focus on creating an outline for a nonfiction book. Nonfiction covers a wide range of topics such as personal development, business, spirituality, memoirs, etc. These are books based on real facts, events, and people.

What is unique about most nonfiction books is that they provide a solution or teach the reader about a topic. Nonfiction books have the ability to lead a reader on a journey to a specific outcome. During the Book Concept Statement process, you defined the reason someone will be picking up your book. Readers of nonfiction are curious to learn something new, have a desire to be transformed, or need a solution to their problem. For example, you might be writing a business book that works to usher in a new form of heart-centered leadership. This means that at the beginning of your book, you need to meet the reader where they are right now. Make it clear that you understand their pain point because you've been there too. Then, as the expert, you can lead them to the solution because you overcame the same challenge.

Memoirs are slightly different in that they don't provide a problem and solution, but these books do follow a transformative story. When outlining for a memoir, consider the journey you are taking the reader on and what they are going to learn about you and your life along the way. How you choose to showcase the events that unfolded in your life's story will be helpful to keep in mind as you enter the outlining process. You want readers to finish reading the book having had a specific positive experience. Hopefully, the process of creating a Book Concept Statement has helped you become clear on what that experience will be. Then, it's about looking at what information a reader needs to know first, second, and third to understand your life's experience. For many creative nonfiction and memoir books that are story-driven, it can be helpful to frame the story as if it were a novel.

No matter which style of nonfiction you are writing, it boils down to this point: Your story needs to have a beginning, middle, and an impactful end.

The outline for your book can be thought of as a staircase. Each chapter is a new step along the path that you've created and encourages the reader to walk down as each chapter presents a concept or life event that builds upon the other. Eventually, this staircase leads readers to the top of the staircase, also known as the solution or satisfying ending.

To help you get a sense of the high-level journey you are taking readers on, I invite you to take a few moments to reflect on the following questions:

- Who was I before my story started?
- What happened that changed my life/me?
- Who am I as a result of these events?

Once you have a strong sense of the beginning, middle, and end of your book from these answers, you have created signposts to help frame your story. These signposts become destinations that you can connect by creating a chapter-by-chapter outline for your book.

At this stage, many authors find it helpful to list out all the stories or pieces of information they want to include in their book. If you are a visual learner, you can take a stack of notecards and write out all the stories that you have in mind and lay them out on a table. Then, you can move them around to see what order you want to present them to the reader in. If you are writing a memoir or a story that is based on chronological events in your life, be careful not to get stuck in a series of "and then..." events. While it can be helpful to know an order of events, it's more important to organize personal stories and experiences from the lessons learned than get too caught up in telling readers that "this happened and then this happened..." Focus instead on the key takeaway that connects back to why a reader will be interested in picking up your book.

Once you have a sense of which stories or life events you want to share, you can begin to break them down into chapters. Each chapter in your book should serve a purpose and move your story forward. Each chapter will build upon the previous while setting up the stage for the next.

To help you frame the purpose behind each chapter, use the following set of questions for a nonfiction book:

- What is the purpose of the chapter?
- What will make up the main content of the chapter?
- What might be a powerful first sentence to capture the reader's attention and set the tone for the chapter topic?
- What anecdotes, testimonials, or stories can I tell?
- What is the key takeaway for the reader?
- Provide any next steps or points of reflection for the reader.

Repeat this exercise for each chapter. As you start to see the progression of chapters, you can revisit your book's theme and your Book Concept Statement to see if you are hitting the mark. These tools are there to help you frame your story in a way that is engaging and compelling to the reader. These tools also help you deliver on the promise of your book so that readers don't become disappointed at the end of your book.

As you define the purpose behind each chapter, you will have a complete chapter-by-chapter outline mapped out for your nonfiction book. Great work! This will provide a bird's-eye view of your book's contents that will help to focus your writing sessions. As this outline comes together, ask yourself these questions:

- Am I capturing what I set out to do?
- Are there any holes in my logic or story?
- Is there anything I left out that the reader would benefit from knowing?

Taking this chapter-by-chapter approach to outlining a nonfiction book will not only show you what you need to write, but it will also help you articulate what the book is about so that readers understand the value of picking up your book. This process will also highlight areas of opportunity for collecting anecdotes, research, case studies, or testimonials, and where they can be plugged into your book to support your story and help to provide important context for your reader.

Another helpful tool to keep in mind for a nonfiction book is the use of book parts and chapter sections. If it adds value to your book, you can break it up into parts. For example, if you are writing a business book, the sections might look like: Starting a Business, Running a Business, Managing People. Within each of these sections, the chapters included would focus on different aspects of the topic. This can be a helpful way to frame your beginning, middle, and end.

Using sections with bolded titles within chapters—as I have done throughout this book—can be helpful to take larger concepts or action steps and break them down. This also provides the reader with a moment of pause as they digest what you are presenting in the chapter. These are not requirements for a nonfiction book, but rather options to further help you frame your ideas. If your nonfiction book isn't better served with sections or chapter breaks, then there is no need to include them. If you are leaning towards including sections or parts within your book, you can define them as you outline or evaluate them as you move into the editing process later. What is most important is that you have a clear and defined reason for including each chapter in your book.

When I coach authors, one of the first places I see nonfiction authors get stuck is with the introduction. Not all books require an introduction, but if you plan to include one, I recommend writing this last. If you start by writing your introduction, many authors struggle because the book hasn't taken form yet. It's hard to set the stage for a play that hasn't been scripted yet. This is why I recommend writing the introduction last. This allows you to confidently align it with the book's main message, key takeaways, and overarching themes once the book has taken shape.

An outline is a structure that provides the flexibility to adapt as needed throughout the writing process. A strong outline sets the foundation for a clear and cohesive book. You can choose to get as granular with the details as you need to. Or you can decide to keep it to a higher-level overview. Neither way is right nor wrong. It's all about getting to a place where you feel confident enough and ready to sit down and write.

Now, I invite you to create your outline to help bring intention and organization to your ideas.

Fiction Book Outlining

In this section, we'll focus on creating an outline for a fiction book. Within the overarching genre of fiction, there are many subgenres. These are novels based on fictitious characters and situations that can range from sci-fi and fantasy to romance and children's books.

The magic of fiction books is their ability to transport us, to create worlds that either reflect our own or create entirely new ones. Fiction books entertain us and often allow a part of ourselves to be seen through the experiences of others. This emotional resonance often happens on a subconscious level for the reader. As a writer, being able to tap into the emotional core of what it is to be human is what makes readers love your book—even if they wouldn't name it as such. What makes fiction unique is the ability to write from an imaginative place that explores universal human emotions and experiences.

To intentionally accomplish this, it starts with an outline. There are many different outline approaches for fiction, so I invite you to explore what works best for you. Many writers—myself included—love to use the three-act structure. For me, the three-act structure approach to outlining strikes the perfect balance of providing a clear structure while allowing creativity and inspiration to emerge as you write. The three-act structure provides the key mile markers that will help you meet reader expectations, while allowing your creativity to emerge as you write. It is a framework that can keep your story cohesive and purposeful while allowing you to write from the seat of your pants along the way. The best part is that you can make the outline as detailed as you'd like, down to each scene within a chapter, or you can keep it high-level by defining the core events while allowing the rest to unfold as you write.

The three-act structure has a long history in storytelling and has been a foundational principle in dramatic writing and playwriting for centuries, consisting of a beginning, middle, and end. Today, the three-act structure remains a widely used and effective tool for outlining and organizing stories, not only in traditional forms but also in contemporary novels, screenplays, and other creative works. Its enduring appeal lies in its ability to create a balanced and engaging narrative flow that keeps readers captivated. The three-act structure is a proven framework for outlining novels.

For a fiction book, the three-act structure takes shape with the following framework:

- Act 1: The Setup
- Act 2: Confrontation and Development
- Act 3: Resolution and Climax

Let's take a closer look at what these acts include and how you can start to shape your book idea using this outline structure:

Act 1: The Setup

The first act of your novel serves as the foundation upon which your story will be built. It introduces the main characters, their goals, and the world they inhabit. Additionally, Act 1 establishes the story's central conflict, setting the stage for the ensuing journey. This can be achieved with the following three elements:

- *Establishing the Status Quo:* Begin by introducing your protagonist and their ordinary world. We want to learn more about how life is now while also getting the sense that everything isn't alright.

- *Inciting Incident:* Shake up your protagonist's world with an event that disrupts their routine and propels them into the main conflict.

- *Rising Action:* As your protagonist embarks on their journey, they encounter obstacles and conflicts that test their resolve. This section of Act 1 builds tension, leading up to the first major turning point.

Act 2: Confrontation and Development

Act 2 is the longest section of your novel, comprising approximately forty percent of the story. This act is where the protagonist faces escalating challenges, encounters allies and enemies, and undergoes significant character development. Here are the four areas to consider for Act 2:

- *First Pinch Point:* This introduces a significant setback or event that reminds the protagonist of the main conflict's severity. This pinch point injects a renewed sense of urgency into the story. It usually presents a point of no return. Meaning, the protagonist can't just say "Never mind," and return to their life as it was before. They have to keep moving forward.

- *Rising Stakes and Complications:* As Act 2 progresses, the protagonist should face escalating obstacles, each more challenging than the last.
- *Midpoint and Revelation:* At the middle of your novel, introduce a pivotal event that alters the protagonist's perception, leading to a new understanding of the central conflict.

Act 3: Resolution and Climax

The final act of your novel is where all the threads of your story converge. It brings the narrative to a satisfying conclusion, answering the central questions raised throughout the book and includes:

- *Preparing for the Climax:* In the early stages of Act 3, the protagonist should regroup, gather their allies, and devise a final plan to overcome the main conflict.
- *Climactic Sequence:* The climax is the most intense and pivotal part of your story. It's the ultimate test for your protagonist, where they confront the antagonist or the central conflict head-on. This is the resolution point of the story.
- *Finale:* After the climax, allow for a period of reflection and resolution. Tie up loose ends, provide closure for your characters, and offer a glimpse into their lives.

You can see from this outlining process that you can simply define these nine elements of your story, and you'll have an outline! It doesn't have to be more complicated than that. These provide the key milestones for you to write toward. With this framework, you can craft a well-structured novel with engaging characters, escalating tension, and a satisfying resolution. This ensures the reader's expectations are met and key milestones are delivered upon.

I will say that when I first learned about the three-act structure, I felt a little heartbroken. I thought that writers just sat down and wrote a plot-filled book. This structure felt formulaic, and I had resistance at first. If you are feeling the same, I get it. Once you see this structure, it is hard to unsee it in books and movies. But that is what also makes it so powerful. It wouldn't be a story worth telling if it didn't follow a rhythm that makes the story flow. We've all had someone try to verbally tell us a story that is a string of "and then," which is the fastest way to tune out any story. The three-act structure becomes a guide for helping you weave together the theme of the story with the action, setting, and character development.

The period of time during which your story takes place provides the reader with a snapshot into your main character's world. And it wouldn't be a story worth telling if this weren't a dramatic or impactful period of their life. Readers expect that this window of time is being captured because the story matters and has meaning. This is why those writing creative nonfiction or memoirs can also approach outlining using the three-act structure. In this case, the author is generally the main character.

Let's look at how the famous story of *Wonder Woman* fits into the three-act structure framework.[14]

Outline Example: Fiction

In the story of *Wonder Woman*, we meet Diana, an Amazon warrior raised on the hidden island of Themyscira. She believes her destiny is to end war by defeating Ares, the god of war. When Steve Trevor, a WWI spy, crashes on the island, Diana learns about the ongoing global conflict and decides to leave her home to stop it. She journeys to the frontlines, convinced that killing Ares will restore peace. Along the way, Diana faces the brutality of war and begins to question her belief in humanity's inherent goodness. In the climactic battle, she discovers that while Ares influences humans, their choices for good or evil come from within. Accepting the complexity of human nature, Diana chooses to fight for love and hope, vowing to inspire humanity to be better despite their flaws.

How does this story fit into the three-act structure? Let's break it down:

Act 1: The Setup

- *Status Quo:* On Themyscira, young Diana trains in secret under her aunt Antiope, dreaming of becoming a warrior. The Amazons are guardians of humanity, tasked with protecting the world from Ares, the god of war.
- *Inciting Incident:* Steve Trevor, a WWI spy, crashes his plane near the island, pursued by German soldiers. Diana saves him, and after a battle, she learns of the ongoing global war. Steve tells her of a deadly weapon being developed that could kill millions.
- *Rising Action:* Believing Ares is behind the war, Diana decides to leave Themyscira to confront him and end the conflict. She takes the Godkiller sword, shield, and lasso, crossing the threshold into the world of men with Steve as her guide.

Act 2: The Confrontation

- *First Pinch Point:* In London, Diana struggles to adapt to human society but remains determined. She and Steve assemble a team and head to the frontlines to stop General Ludendorff and Dr. Maru, whom she believes are influenced by Ares.
- *Rising Stakes:* Diana's idealism is tested as she witnesses the horrors of war. Despite her heroic actions, human suffering and moral ambiguity begin to challenge her faith in humanity's inherent goodness.

- *Midpoint:* In a powerful moment on the battlefield, Diana defies orders and charges across No Man's Land, inspiring the Allied troops to push forward. This marks her emergence as a hero, but her belief that Ares is the sole cause of war remains unshaken.
- *Second Pinch Point:* Diana kills Ludendorff, thinking he is Ares, but the war doesn't end. This shatters her belief that defeating Ares will automatically restore peace.

Act 3: The Resolution

- *Preparing for the Climax:* Ares reveals himself and confronts Diana, trying to convince her that humanity is irredeemable and that she should join him in destroying them. During their battle, Diana learns the truth about her own identity: she is a demigod, the daughter of Zeus, and the true Godkiller.
- *Climactic Sequence:* Diana realizes that while Ares influences humanity, humans have free will and are capable of both great evil and great good. Inspired by Steve's self-sacrifice to destroy the deadly weapon, she chooses to fight for love, hope, and the possibility of a better future.
- *Finale/Resolution:* Ares is defeated, and the war ends, but Diana now understands that peace is not simple or guaranteed. She stays in the world of men, dedicating herself to protecting humanity and inspiring them to rise above their flaws.

From this example, you can see how the three-act structure can be applied to most stories. I invite you to think about a recent movie you've watched to see if you can identify these key events throughout the story. This outlining framework allows you to build up tension and suspense while inviting your main character to grow so that they can get what they want or need.

Now, it's time for you to outline your book and see how it feels. I recommend doing this and then letting it sit for a day or two so that you can let the ideas land where they need to and reorganize them as you receive additional inspiration.

Character and Story Arc: Fiction and Nonfiction

No matter the outline approach you decide to take, it is important to remember that a human-driven story is one that is going to connect deeply with your readers. That is why the arc of the story—the journey from the beginning to the end—is important to spend time on.

For fiction writers, this is done by focusing on who your character was at the beginning of your book while having a clear understanding of who they will become by the end of your book. The same applies to nonfiction writers, only the main character is either you or your reader. The main character needs to experience growth and change in ways that get them closer to what they want.

While the outlining process does hit on elements around character development, it can be helpful to hone in on how your main character will react, respond, and transform throughout your book. I will use the phrase main character or character to refer to a fictional character for fiction and the author or reader for nonfiction. This is what creates that subconscious emotional connection with readers. By having a clearly defined story arc for the character, readers can build an emotional connection—be it good or bad—with your characters. Not only that, but readers will root for your characters. This is the fuel that will keep them engaged and reading throughout all the plot elements.

Your main character's internal conflict becomes the heartbeat of the story. This internal conflict—often a deep struggle between their desires, fears, beliefs, or identity—directly impacts the external actions they take in the plot. By mapping these two layers (internal conflict and plot) together, writers can create a cohesive, resonant story where the character's emotional growth aligns with the story's progression.

Think of it like a layered map:

- *The internal conflict* represents the emotional journey—the invisible line that guides how the character grows, evolves, or resists change.

- The *plot* represents the external journey—the visible events and actions that test and challenge the character. These have been outlined using the three-act structure.

When these two layers are intertwined, the external events force the character to confront their internal struggle, while the internal struggle shapes how the character reacts to those events. This alignment keeps the story compelling and ensures that every plot point has emotional stakes. Readers remember how a book made them *feel*, and they don't always recall all the plot points. That's why we often refer to books as "I liked that book!" or "I didn't like that book." We want our books to evoke a positive feeling state.

How do you achieve this? Start by mapping out your character's internal conflict alongside the plot. This ensures that every external challenge also has emotional stakes. Ask yourself:

- Who was this character at the beginning of the story?
- What do they want?
- How does this event challenge the character's beliefs, fears, or desires?
- Who do they have to become to get what they want?
- How does the character's reaction to this event reveal their growth or resistance to change?

The best characters are layered—filled with strengths, flaws, and desires that feel authentic. As the writer, it is your job to bring your characters to life and draw readers into their journeys, creating emotional resonance. Internal conflict is the heart of a good story. When your character is torn between desires or beliefs, it creates tension that keeps readers hooked. This might look like a desire for success versus self-destructive tendencies or loneliness versus a fear of connection.

Spend some time thinking about your main character. How do all their flaws, wants, and plot events intersect to create both internal and external growth and change?

You can also use these questions to help develop your supporting cast of characters. How do their decisions, flaws, and reactions create resistance or push your main character to grow?

To create dynamic characters that create emotional resonance with readers, make them as human as possible. Have fun with this!

Let the Outlining Begin

It's time to take that idea you have for a book and start outlining it! This is akin to gathering all 5,000 puzzle pieces and placing them in the center of the table. Don't focus on the result just yet. It starts with finding the corner pieces.

You don't have to know where all the pieces go right away. You just have to seek out the next piece. This process isn't about outlining a perfect and flawless book. It is about creating a springboard to the journey you're taking readers on and creating a space where your writing can bloom and begin to take shape.

Many times, during the outlining process, we start with one story idea, but as we start writing, we realize we need to make a specific pit stop or a right-hand turn to visit an important site. That's okay; the process of writing a book isn't linear. The most important piece is that the groundwork for your book has been accomplished, and your creative process has the room to unfold. An outline serves as a tool that can hold the structure of your story while remaining flexible enough to adapt as needed. There is often a duality between having clarity on your story's structure while knowing that you may have to let go of some well-intended pieces to make the book flow.

Allow your outline to be a living, breathing document that can be updated and shifted as needed. That is the exciting part of the writing journey—you never know what you will find or learn along the way. As you expand, get to know your characters, or tap back into a transformative time in your life, you will gain more insight into yourself and what the reader needs to know next.

Start by testing out the outlining method that works for you. This doesn't have to be perfect; it's a guiding framework, not a contractual obligation. An outline provides a 10,000-foot view to see what information is presented when and what pieces may need more context or what plot points need to be resolved. Take the time to let the outline arrive at a place where you feel you have planned enough to start. Remember, an outline is the flowerpot where your story can be planted and begin to thrive. It sets the foundation for a clear and cohesive book that readers will love while paving a path for you to capture your ideas to focus your creative efforts.

CHAPTER

7

Writing with Mindfulness

To write with mindfulness is to surrender to the process. When you slow down and accept the process, your words have the space to deepen their meaning. When we set a large goal for ourselves, such as writing a book, it can be tempting to put all our energy into it like a new gym membership in January, only to find that we overextended ourselves and want to quit before February.

Bringing mindfulness into our writing practice can make all the difference between *starting* to write a book and *finishing* a book. Mindfulness can take on a different shape for each writer. The intent behind bringing mindfulness into your writing practice is to take the time to create a thoughtful approach to how you are going to write your book. It isn't about taking action just to take action. In this case, it's about taking intentional action toward your dream of writing and publishing a book that is sustainable over time.

Writing is just that—a practice. It is a muscle to be developed. Creating a writing practice is like creating a yoga practice. If you've had a yoga or meditation practice, you know that it can ebb and flow. It is a practice we can return to that helps to strengthen our bodies, minds, and spirits. Writing is the same. It is similar to yoga in that there are many ways to practice. Writing can look different during each session, and it doesn't always have to be the same. Some days, it might be sitting down to write. Some days, it might be taking a walk and observing the world around you. Other days, it might be doing research for your book. Whatever it looks like, it all counts. Every step you take, every word you write—it all counts as progress. Not all days look the same. It's all about embracing where you are each session. There is no forcing or pushing to be better or to do more than you did last time you engaged in the practice. It is all about being present. It is about doing what is in front of you. As I started developing my writing muscle, I found that the more I wrote, the more the light of my soul started to shine brighter and brighter.

Even with an outline in hand, the act of writing can often feel like the hardest part because it asks us to show up over and over again. We don't just sit down to write once and then we've reached our writing goal. That's the thing about the creative process; it requires an element of surrender, which feels counterintuitive to taking action. Writing does require the action of putting words on the page, but by allowing our creative process to unfold, we can bring a level of mindfulness that nurtures us through the process. It is about setting the right intentions for our writing process and letting go of controlling every element, knowing that it may be different than what we expected. The writing process is birthing something new, and everyone's birth is unique. The writing process won't always be linear. It can be messy, but the more you can be open, the more the words can flow. When our intent is clear, we can mindfully move through the writing process in a way that is a pleasant experience.

Mindfulness can deepen creativity. When we approach the creative process with a sense of intentionality, we reduce the need to stress and force the words to come. Instead, we provide our creativity with the space to deepen and expand in ways we could never have planned for. Writing is an organic process that asks us to both respect it and guide it. Hence why it helps to have an outline as a container to keep our ideas focused while having the flexibility to explore what our story needs to become as we write.

Additionally, developing a writing practice provides the space for your book to take shape. A writing practice is actively creating the time to work on your book and put words on the page. When we remain consistent, we eventually have enough words to shape an entire book. I find that to be a mind-bogglingly cool concept. We all have access to the same words, but we can each uniquely create a world of our own and then invite people into it. Maybe that's why I like hanging out with writers so much!

The thing about progress is that it never takes as long as we think it will. Every time I sit down to write, even for ten to fifteen minutes, I often accomplish more than I anticipated. By engaging with my writing, I have overcome and quieted any resistance, which fuels an aliveness within that connects me deeper to my work, and I feel energized by my writing progress.

Developing a writing practice is a structure that offers accountability and the space to allow your writing journey to unfold. After all, a blank page provides nothing to work with. A writing practice is all about getting words on the page while maintaining the flexibility that allows the practice to be what it needs to be. It is about being willing to write terribly and clean it up later. When you have words on the page, you have something that can be shaped into your final story.

By taking the time to get intentional with how you want your writing practice to look and feel, you are taking a mindful approach to writing. This may feel as if you are slowing down, but you are, in fact, creating a container that will help you build momentum with your writing. It's about being present—tapping into what you need to support your creative process, staying consistent, and allowing the words to flow, even if they are extremely messy at first.

How to Establish a
Mindful Writing Practice

To create a mindful writing practice, it starts with knowing what you are aiming for. For myself and many of the authors I've worked with, creating a target end goal helps to direct writing efforts and allows for reverse engineering how to get there. I prefer to use a total word count as an end target. With a total word count in mind for your book, you can then establish how many words you want and can reasonably write per month, week, or day. When it comes to determining the total word count for your book, there are a few industry standards for the length of books based on genre:

- Nonfiction: 50,000 words
- Fiction: 90,000 words
- Children's Books: 500–1,000 words

These are not hard and fast rules, and if your book is slightly over or under these numbers, that is okay too. This is especially true for your first draft, when you may end up under or over on the total number of words. In my first draft, I tend to write below the total word count I'm aiming for, knowing that during the editing process, I will expand on descriptions of places, scenes, case studies, etc. The point of a word count is to help you know what a completed manuscript is for you.

Once you have established your word count, you need to decide when you would like to have your book written by. Is it six months from now? Two years from now? This timeline allows you to further break down how much you would like to write during each month, week, or writing session—whichever is most helpful for you. For example, if you want to write a nonfiction book in six months, you'll divide 50,000 words by six months, which equals 8,333.33 words per month. Let's call it 8,333 for simple math. Next, you can break this down further to establish how many words that requires you to write per week by taking 8,333 and dividing it by four, which equals 2,085 words per week. Next, you can identify how many writing sessions you will plan per week. If you are planning to have four writing sessions per week, that means you would need to divide 2,085 by four, which equals 520 words—so, you would need to write 520 words during each of those four writing sessions.

Now, ask yourself, does writing 520 words four times per week for the next six months feel doable? If the answer is yes, then great!

If the answer is no, then ask yourself how you might make some adjustments so that it does feel doable. Can you extend the timeline to eight or twelve months? Could you add one more writing session per week? Play around with this until you feel like the goal is achievable.

At the onset of working together, an author I was coaching was on a mission to write the first draft of her novel within three months. While not impossible, I quickly saw how this author had packed her already full schedule with large three-hour blocks of writing either at the beginning of her day—which required getting up at 4:30 am—or late at night, literally burning the midnight oil. As a coach, I love an action-oriented individual, but I also understand the importance of setting realistic goals. When I checked in with this writer to assess if this was *really* realistic for her schedule, her response was, "I'll make it work! I'm ready to write this damn book!" I take my lead from each author, so I enthusiastically supported her as she embarked on her new writing practice.

Two weeks later, during our check-in, I could tell that her enthusiasm was waning and barely evident. As we addressed what hadn't worked with her "make-it-work-plan," it came to light that this book had been sitting on her heart for more than a decade, and she felt that in order to finally get it out of her system and onto the page, she needed to sit down and force herself to make it happen. While this was hard for her to admit, this was also a breakthrough. By trying to force words onto the page, this author was robbing herself of the joy of finally writing her book. She wasn't allowing her book to take form in the most impactful way by slowing down and getting intentional with how she wanted to feel as she wrote her book.

Together, we created a plan that allowed her to flow more when it came to her writing. We started by extending her timeline for writing her book. She was able to understand that it was more important to take a little longer to have a finished book that she had enjoyed writing than to push for an unlikely deadline that would have made her give up altogether. During each coaching call, we would revisit her outline, and she would decide which chapter she felt most inspired to write next. Over time, she established that she preferred writing a chapter per month, which gave her the space to get really creative with her writing and space out her writing sessions when she had more creativity earlier in the day—thankfully, after seven in the morning. This author was able to make peace with the process by focusing on her intention, which allowed her writing practice to move from pushing through to writing from a flow state.

Creating a writing practice isn't about forcing ourselves to sit down and churn out words. It's about creating a sustainable writing practice that can nurture our creativity. The opposite of the flow state is force. Pushing and forcing ourselves to sit down to write four chapters sounds painful. It's the same with bending over to touch our toes. We reach for the space that we can; otherwise, we might injure ourselves. That doesn't feel good. It's about making progress, even if that means only getting five words or one hundred words on the page. Showing up to put any words on the page feels great because it is building momentum. There are times to encourage ourselves to write, but we never want to feel like we are forcing it.

That is why taking a mindful approach to your writing process can inspire creativity and reduce stress. It helps you break each writing session down into an achievable accomplishment instead of feeling like you need to write an entire book in a weekend. Often, the writing process can be thought of as this grand sweeping idea that magically appears on the page, but in reality, it's a process of honoring what we need and building word by word. When we create a space for progress over perfection, we encourage our creativity to step forward and flourish.

Once you understand your total word count and what feels achievable for each writing session, I recommend writing this down in a place that is visible where you write. I also recommend taking this a step further by scheduling your writing sessions into your calendar, right now. Writing is now a priority. It is not something you will get to when you have time. You've just created a path for yourself. I invite you to create the time to walk down it. If you haven't done so already, now is the time to define your word count and break it down into monthly, weekly, or daily writing goals as it feels right for you. Clarity comes by doing. So don't get hung up on having the perfect goal. You'll discover your next step as you jump into the writing process.

Creating a Mindful Writing Practice

Now that you have an understanding of what you are aiming for when it comes to your word count, let's design your writing sessions. It is one thing to know what your writing goal is, and it is another thing to know *how* you are going to accomplish it. Start by asking yourself these questions:

- What would an ideal writing session look like for me?
- What will make me most excited to show up for each writing session?

Creating a mindful writing practice is about designing what your writing sessions will look, taste, smell, sound, and feel like. As you explore your writing practice, there is an opportunity to learn to feel what it is you need, aside from reaching a specific word count goal for the day. It starts with finding the right sensory signals for your brain that say, "Hey, we're moving into writing mode now." Start by considering what will support you the most to get words on the page. Consider what these signals might be for you:

- Is it making a cup of coffee or tea?
- Is it journaling?
- Is it going for a walk?
- Is it finding a new coffee shop to work in?

- Is it hitting play on your favorite playlist?
- Is it lighting your favorite scented candle?
- Is it sitting with the sensations of impostor syndrome or self-doubt?
- Is it meditating?

It could be telling your partner, family, or roommates that you need thirty uninterrupted minutes. I don't, however, recommend telling your cat. Extensive videos on social media have shown that they are *more* likely to lie on your keyboard with advanced warning!

This isn't about showing up perfectly; it's about showing up *consistently* for your dreams. Whatever you need, honor it. This is where mindfulness can be a powerful tool in fueling the creative process. Whichever way you choose to engage with the word mindfulness is up to you. It might be a matter of reviewing your why for writing the book before sitting down to write. It could be meditation or prayer. It could be moving your body. It could be taking a bath. An artist might doddle before ever putting a brush against a canvas. There is no right way to do this.

Choose one or two signals that will allow you to move toward writing. Everyone's creative process is different. As you start to engage with your writing practice, it is important to remember that every session may look different. I know for myself, there are some days when the words just flow. On other days, I need to move my body before I can write. Some days, I need to journal and meditate before I feel open enough to engage in the act of writing. Being a writer is a vulnerable act. It takes a lot of courage to keep showing up—especially when you don't want to—and keep creating. The intention with which you sit down to write can be felt and come across on the page. Why not make this process as enjoyable as possible?

A tricky element that can emerge is that inspiration doesn't always strike at the exact same time every day. I know I've had some of my best ideas while in the shower. So many, in fact, that I had to buy washable markers so that I could capture the brilliant dialogue between two characters. When we set a goal, our brains will go into problem-solving mode to find a path forward toward our goals, even if we aren't consciously working on it. Doing nothing is productive; your brain will actively work on it in the background. If you find yourself writing sentences or ideas in your Notes app or recording voice memos in between writing sessions to capture this creativity as best you can, then allow that to unfold. You can begin your next writing session by taking those notes and adding them to your manuscript.

If you do find yourself capturing notes here, there, and everywhere, or you are unable to capture the great idea you had while driving, know that the most important pieces that need to be included in your book will come back to you. Allow inspiration to pop up when it needs to and trust that it will continue to show up in your writing sessions.

Does writing dialogue on my shower wall like a psychopath count as a writing session? You bet it does! Being mindful of what you need in the process does not mean you aren't being productive. It means you're choosing what you need and trusting the process.

Your story can consume a lot of energy trying to free itself from your mind. It's important that writing doesn't become a drain but rather a well of inspiration. To tap into this spring of inspiration, you must not only trust yourself, but you must also be honest with what you need when it comes to making writing a sacred practice.

An author I coached had designed a writing practice that had short writing sprints of ten to fifteen minutes per day. While she was able to stay consistent with these sprints, she found she was becoming addicted to the feeling of getting words on the page, regardless of whether they were meaningful or helped move her story forward. After two months of checking all the boxes on her writing sessions, she confessed that she felt lost in her story and had no idea if anything she had been writing over the past eight weeks would even be usable in her book.

Through coaching, we explored that her anxiety of not meeting her writing session goals had eclipsed her desire to write a book. She had become so addicted to the process of checking to-dos off her list that she had completely lost sight of why she was writing her book. As a planner and maker of daily to-do lists, I can relate to this! The satisfaction of checking things off the list does feel good. The key here is to check in frequently on your intention. Together, this author and I revisited her why for writing. We also revisited the purpose behind her book. Once we reconnected with her larger picture and she recommitted to why she was doing what she was doing, we revisited how she approached these writing sessions.

Since she had fifteen-minute increments to write in, we decided that the first five minutes would be spent slowing down in a mindful way to allow her brain to focus on what would be the next right step in her writing based on her outline. These five minutes were spent on tapping back into her why and being present with her creativity rather than pushing to get as many words on the page as possible. Then, the following ten minutes were spent writing words that would be used in her book. After test-driving this new approach for two weeks, she came back to me having made more writing progress than she had the previous month. By slowing down, tapping into her why, creating an outline, and being mindful about how she wanted to move forward, she was able to make even more progress than hustling to get words on the page and check off a completed writing session.

If this is the writing experience you would like to have, before diving into your writing session, take a few moments to ground yourself, tune in, and open the creative channel with intention.

1. Find a comfortable seat—perhaps in your writing chair.
2. Check in with your body: What sensations are present? Are you holding tension anywhere? See if you can soften it, even by 10%.
3. If it feels right, close your eyes.
4. Take three deep, intentional breaths, letting each exhale bring you into the present moment.
5. Gently roll your shoulders. Notice the sensation of your feet on the floor, the weight of your body in the chair.
6. Bring your attention to your writing: What story, idea, or expression is calling to you today? What would feel most fulfilling to explore?
7. Take three more deep breaths.
8. Open your eyes. Roll your wrists, shake out any lingering tension.

Now, begin. The page is ready for you.

Being mindful with your writing practice means having flexibility while being present. It is to be present, in this moment now, without judgment. That means not shaming yourself for not doing laundry. That means not judging the words that you put onto the page that didn't land the way they did in your head. Being present means you're aware of your body, mind, and feelings in this moment *without* trying to change them. This mindful approach to writing is grounding because it helps us slow down and creates space to become more present. That is one of the most valuable skills an author can develop to sink into a satisfying writing session.

My invitation to you is to have fun and experiment with your writing practice. It doesn't have to be perfect, just consistent. The beginning of your writing practice development may come with some testing and learning. If you've ever made pottery before, you know there are times when you've sculpted a mug or vase, and it just doesn't look like you wanted it to. So, you smush it up and leave the clay for the next project. As a writer, you are sculpting a book, and not every writing session will produce the most eloquent words you've ever written. With each writing session and each word placed on the page, you are getting closer to a final manuscript. There will be times to slow down and let your writing and thoughts integrate, while there will be other times when you can't type fast enough.

If, along the way, you find that consistency wavering, that is okay. Life happens when you're writing a book. If you miss a writing session, don't beat yourself up. What is most important is that you show up again for the next one you have scheduled. During that next session, it isn't about forcing yourself to make up for what you didn't write in the last session. Drop the self-judgment and keep going. The goal is to show up and meet your goal for *that* session. If you get more done, great! If not, you still showed up. Showing up is what builds your writing muscle and fuels your motivation to keep making progress word by word.

The writing practice isn't meant to be constrictive. It is designed to be a container to allow your words to flow. If you find that the writing practice isn't supporting that flow, then trust yourself to allow the flow of your words to come. The most important thing is that you're consistent and making progress, even if it looks messy and only makes sense to you. Not writing the book is not an option.

As we've explored, creating a writing practice shouldn't be a rigid exercise; it needs to be a consistent space that you can hold for yourself to keep making progress toward your writing desires. If you've tried one or two things and feel stuck, try asking yourself, What is the experience I want to have as I write my book? There will always be opportunities to find excuses and reasons not to write, but you get to decide which you engage with more.

The foundational work you have been doing here by creating an outline, establishing your word count, and creating a mindful writing practice might feel as if you're behind on the writing process. But let me tell you, these steps are what make the difference between a writer who never finishes their book and a writer who publishes their book. You're setting the foundation for the success that you want. That takes courage and patience—and you're doing it—bravo! I'm proud of you for honoring what you need in the writing process.

The key is to become obsessed with the creative process and persistent in reaching your writing goals. Every time you sit down to write, it may look different. Learning to trust yourself with your writing, even when it makes sense to no one else— potentially even yourself—is an act of self-love. Writing is a sacred practice that asks you to show up for yourself and follow what lights you up. Trust that the right ideas are coming through. Trust that the right words for your book will flow because you are clear on why you are writing this book and the impact it will have. Surrender to the process and trust yourself to follow what is needed in each moment to write the book that sits on your heart.

Writing from Your Truth

Your voice in its truest expression is the bridge between your story and the hearts of your readers. By exploring your unique expression of your ideas, stories, and perspective, you are honoring the story that sits in your heart. By honoring what you know to be true and real, your voice can shine through, and the writing can flow.

When you can access what makes you unique, you are writing from your true creative essence—that is, writing from your innermost truth. To write authentically from our truth, we have to allow ourselves to be where we are without self-judgment and questioning.

Writing became a sacred practice for me when I stopped dancing around what I thought my writing should look and sound like and instead connected with the true meaning behind my words. By dropping the façade, I was able to honor what lights me up while being in service to others. Less than one percent of the words I will have written over the course of my lifetime will become published works, and that is exactly how I want it to be. For me, writing is about self-exploration, healing, and exploring how I can become a better writer while inviting others to do the same. Not all my self-expression needs to be consumed by others—having a sacred writing practice means that some words remain sacred to myself. However, the words that do get published are going to be meaningful and capture my truth in a way that lets my voice shine and land with those who need to hear them.

If writing from your truth brings up fear—I see this a lot with memoir writers—take a moment to assess what that fear is trying to do. Often, it wants to protect us from bad reviews or other people's opinions. In the case of memoir writers, there are often key people in their lives who are involved with the story they are telling. Difficult relationships among family members and friends can be challenging to write about. The important thing to focus on is the lesson that came out of these situations. Writing isn't about blaming or shaming the people in our lives, but about exposing our point of view and our experiences in the service of a lesson. If you are writing in the memoir genre, writing from your truth is paramount. If this is too difficult, it might be worth asking if your story could be fictionalized. Either way, it is a valid concern to be writing about other people in your book. At the end of the day, writing from your truth means sharing your experiences in a way that could open up healing conversations. After all, no two humans ever have the same experience of an event or situation—two sides to every story and all that.

Writing from your truth in your authentic voice means showing up despite it feeling scary. Your voice is made up of your tone, vocabulary, perspective, authenticity, and rhythm and flow of sentences. In other words, your voice is how your story sounds when it's being told. It's you on the page, and no one else can replicate that. Giving your voice life on the page might sound easy, but in practice, it can be challenging to let your true, authentic voice flow when your inner voice is telling you that no one will listen. This is a great time to remind yourself that you are growing, expanding, and becoming the writer you were always meant to be. This is not an overnight transformation.

When we first sit down to write, the words may not land the way we intended in our heads. As writers, we can easily start to shame ourselves for not being better writers or allow impostor syndrome—the feeling that our writing will never be good enough—to make us think that we should quit altogether. Not today, writer!

Here is the thing: Your first draft is going to suck. It's going to be messy. It's meant to be. The first draft is all about getting some resemblance to the idea you have in your head onto paper so you can mold it into what you envision. This asks us to become obsessed with the process as much as the outcome.

To support you in stepping into your confidence and your true voice, consider the following questions:

- What truth have I been afraid to write?
- If my voice had no filter, what would it say?

Writing from your truth means that you're willing to do the work as you move through the writing process while also allowing yourself to embrace your voice without fear of judgment—from yourself or others. It means being vulnerable and creating a deeper connection with your reader—regardless of the genre you are writing in.

How to Establish Your Voice

Establishing your voice can take time to unfold. In fact, your voice is ever evolving because you are continually growing and expanding over your lifetime. It's never something we find once and that's it. The more you write, the more your voice will evolve.

To connect with readers and inspire them, you have to show up and write from your truest voice. The number one thing that readers can see through is bullshit. Since you are here, reading this book, I know you're not here to write a book full of bull.

Establishing your voice comes through the act of writing. It is something you can nurture and develop as you consistently put pen to paper. Here are a few tips for honing your voice:

- Write like you speak: Play around with humor, introspection, or formality to discover what feels right.
- Study other authors: What makes them stand out? Why are you drawn to them?
- Experiment without pressure: Play around with the length of your sentences and point of view, or look up synonyms for frequently used words.

The goal is to allow yourself to let your story land without filters. It is about getting playful and expanding the edges of your creative container to allow your story to land on the page in a way that honors your intent while connecting to the emotional core of your reader. When we try to contain our message, our voice can fall flat. What ignites our tone, vocabulary, and rhythm and flow of sentences is allowing our truest story to emerge from expansion, not contraction.

Finding Your Flow with Writing

Similar to finding your voice, finding your flow with writing is something that will manifest over time the more you engage with writing. For myself—and for many of the authors I've worked with—flow is achieved when we have clarity on the underlying theme of our book while allowing the words to fall onto the page without judgment. When we are clear on our book's purpose and engaged with our writing process, then the writing begins to flow.

As the purpose of your book develops and your creative process unfolds, you've created a container for the words to flow. Being in flow means you are creating from your truth without judgment. To access your flow, it can be helpful to create for yourself first. How do you want to experience the story you are telling? Set down the need to always have your reader in mind. Create for yourself first, then those who align with your story will find it. Allow yourself to be vulnerable and pour words onto the page. As you continue to show up for yourself and your writing practice, that will build momentum, which creates flow.

That's not to say that there won't be times when the words seem difficult to find. Sometimes the words will be pouring out, and sometimes it will seem harder. Honor both. Neither experience means anything about you as a writer.

Taking a mindful approach to your writing allows for greater presence, which creates an invitation for flow and ease. Here are some tips for getting into a writing flow:

- Reconnect to your *why* for writing the book.
- Engage in your writing practice so your brain knows it is time to focus on writing.

- Engage with prewriting activities like making tea, lighting a candle, or tapping play on your writing soundtrack.
- Focus on one chapter or scene at a time, not the big picture.
- Let go of editing while writing: Flow happens when you trust the process and focus on creating, not correcting.

Creativity and getting in the flow of writing isn't about "finding it." It's about allowing what we already know how to do, but have been conditioned to produce, to occur naturally. Tap into why you are doing this, what you want, and allow that to drive the flow, not the outcome.

Heather was an author I coached who kept getting caught up in a spiral of sessions where words flowed onto the page followed by sessions where she felt like she had to force them on the page. Heather had been working on a novel for years, but she didn't know how to finish her book. After years of trying, she decided to set it down and eventually started writing another book. Only the same thing happened: she was forcing words on the page. She felt lost, confused, and took this as a sign she shouldn't be a writer. After all, what writer can't figure out how to write more than a third of the book? Her forcing and second-guessing had derailed any potential writing progress—Heather's story is not unlike my own.

For years, I would second-guess my ability to write. I thought that I wasn't meant to be a writer because I couldn't sit down and write a book while on vacation. I felt lost, unsure of how to keep moving forward, and I was afraid that I would never see the light at the end of the tunnel. I would take my pages and stuff them into the back of a drawer, hoping that one day the book would magically finish itself.

What changed for me was learning to let the words flow and tap into what it was I wanted to achieve. That started with learning that stories were more than just the plot. That character growth was key for readers to resonate with the story, and that dialogue served a purpose to help inform and move the story forward; it wasn't just there to show that the characters were capable of talking. Or even how nonfiction writers create a path for readers to walk down while also making the content accessible, digestible, and impactful. A lot of imagination, thought, skill, and knowledge go into writing a book. Allowing for space and time to experiment with establishing your writing as you learn new skills will help you find your voice and let your story shine on the page as only your voice can.

Writing a book is a journey, and both your voice and writing flow evolve. The more you write, the more confident you'll feel. The more you can tap into your sincere place of truth, the more your writing style will emerge in a powerful and impactful way. Writing is an opportunity to share from your innermost truth. That means showing up without judgment to produce words on the page, even if fear is sitting next to you. It is through consistently showing up and being honest with our truth and unique voice that we can find flow in our words, allowing them to carry a story's impact.

Editing Is a Magical Refinement Process

Editing is where your book becomes its truest self. While it can be tempting to edit as you write, I encourage you to focus on writing forward as much as you can through your writing practice. The first draft is all about getting your idea out of your head and onto paper. With words on the page, you have something you can refine into its final shape. On the contrary, a blank page provides nothing to work with. The magic of making your writing come alive is through the editing process.

Editing as you write can feed impostor syndrome and delay meaningful writing sessions. It is very tempting to sit down for your perfectly constructed writing session only to spend the entire time correcting and cleaning up what you wrote yesterday. While there may be times when this is a productive use of time, it becomes less productive when you spend all your time editing and not continuing to write your story.

When this happens, take a moment to pause and remind yourself that there will be a lot of time to edit in the future.

Ask yourself, what notes do you need to take down about the writing you have already done thus far so that you can keep moving the story along? This might look like comments in the margins or dropping your ideas into a separate document—I like to call mine the parking lot. Whatever works best for you, I invite you to capture editing notes and allow them to hold their own space while you continue to get the rest of your story onto the page. Becoming stuck in a state of correcting blocks the flow of our words.

Until all the words are dumped onto the page, you won't have the full picture of what the book can be. That means your editing efforts as you write could be doing more harm than help. Just like writing is a journey, editing is also a unique journey.

One of the most commonly asked questions I receive is, *How do I know when I am ready to start the editing process?* There are a few indicators: having reached your word count goal, having written the end, or your story feels as complete as it can be at this stage. You'll know you're ready to start editing when the ideas that have been swirling around in your head are finally on the page.

The first step on the editing journey is to step away—this might sound counterintuitive, but allowing your completed manuscript to sit for a few days, weeks, or even months can do wonders for your editing journey. Coming back to your manuscript with fresh eyes to embark on the editing process is one of the most valuable steps you can take. By allowing time between writing and editing phases, you can usher in a mindset switch. This mindset switch is going from a creative writing process to an analytical editing mode, where each sentence will be scrutinized.

Since the switch from writing to editing takes a change in mindset approach, allowing time between the writing process and the editing process can be the most valuable gift you can give yourself. If the idea of editing makes you cringe, you are not alone. It can feel like a daunting, arduous, and overwhelming process that mimics a wrestling match, only the opponent is your words on the page. For a lot of authors, editing can be another creative process along the writing journey that allows them to refine their story to maximize its impact.

If you are anything like Francesca, an author I worked with during her editing journey, she was dreading the editing process. Francesca's editing process started slowly, one page at a time. There were key areas that Francesca knew she needed to focus on. One area we focused on during our sessions was her dialogue. Within fiction books, dialogue serves to reveal information about the character while moving the story forward. In Francesca's case, there were moments where she had added in dialogue just because it had been a while since any characters had spoken—this is not uncommon, especially for debut novelists.

The joy for Francesca came through when she realized that the editing process allowed her to experiment and explore the craft of writing more deeply. As she learned more about the role of dialogue, she had fun experimenting with not only the purpose behind the dialogue she wrote but also experimenting with adding in emotions and actions that helped to reveal what was really happening with her characters. Just like in real life, what is said is not always what is meant, and our body language can be very telling.

Francesca found joy in being able to spend time during the editing process on how she was able to help her characters become more vibrant and stand out on the page. By the time she published and started receiving book reviews, a number mentioned how her dialogue felt natural but also made readers laugh out loud.

Taking your time during the editing process might feel uncomfortable at first, but as you begin to sculpt and mold your words, the magic starts to unfold. If you allow it, the editing process can be exciting. That's because you get to play around with options and land on the best decision for your book and writing style. And who knows, perhaps like Francesca, you will also find joy in sculpting elements in your book that readers end up loving.

Another factor to consider for editing your book is to invite other people into your process. It can feel scary to share your work—that is to be expected! That is why finding the right partners who not only believe in your work but also provide valuable feedback beyond "I liked it" or "It was good" is a game-changer in bringing forth your completed manuscript. The right partners could be in the form of professional editors, critique groups, or early readers called beta readers. This is where you get to stress test your ideas and receive feedback:

- Is the story you are conveying landing in the way you intended?
- Does your story flow?
- Were there places people got stuck or needed more clarity?

You might also learn the key takeaways that each reader gained to ensure you communicated your book's purpose. Based on this feedback, you can make the necessary adjustments before publishing your book.

Feedback is designed to help you grow, but you do have to develop a filter to help decipher what is helpful input versus noise. Early in my writing career, and before I became an editor, I had no idea there were stages to the editing process. When I heard someone mention a book editor, I always assumed they were talking about an editor who looked for typos. I later learned that editing is like peeling an onion; there are layers to the process. No matter if you are planning to self-edit or work with professional editors, it's important to follow the stages of editing to have the most polished manuscript.

Let's look at the stages of editing:

Developmental Editing

This is the first stop along the editing journey. This is a bird's-eye view of your book's structure, pacing, character development, point of view, plot, and themes. This phase of the editing process ensures that each chapter is in the right place, that characters are introduced at the right time, that there are no plot holes or timeline inconsistencies, and that each story or anecdote you have shared has a purpose and connects to the purpose of the chapter it is in. This is the time to move large pieces of the manuscript around, such as whole chapters or paragraphs. This is the time to cut characters. This is the time to make sure the plot doesn't have any unanswered questions. For nonfiction, this is also the time to ensure that each chapter builds upon the previous and the core themes are carried through, leaving the reader with key takeaways.

This phase of the editing process is about ensuring that the structure of your book will make sense to readers. It isn't about making sure that spelling or grammar are correct; that comes later. This is about making sure the journey you set out to take readers on meets their expectations.

This is the area of editing that I am certified and specialize in. I love working with authors to ensure that their core message and reader experience are landing in the way they wanted. It is about making sure the way in which you have structured your story is presented for maximum reader satisfaction. This is where all the boxes get checked around delivering on the purpose and your *why* behind the book. This is the time to poke and ask questions that could challenge why specific aspects of your book exist and question if they are in the right place. Developmental editing ensures that the foundation of your story and the framing of your house are sturdy and pass inspection. If you jump straight into the copy editing and realize later that you need to make structural changes, you'll have to go back and do the copy editing all over again. So, it's important not to skip this phase so that you don't have to redo work later. Editing isn't just about skipping to the spelling and grammar to meet a publishing target. If you skip this step, it can lead to a faulty book. Readers are smart, and they are more than happy to point out flaws in reviews. This is the time and place to catch any issues before the reader does.

Line Editing

This is the next stop along the editing journey. Now that the structure is in place, it is time to dig into the sentence-level structure. This level of editing focuses on analyzing whether the most effective words have been used to convey a message or thought. This process might involve asking questions such as:

- Is there a better way to say it?
- Could it be said in fewer words?
- Is the appropriate context in place?

All these types of questions are answered during the line editing process. It ensures that every word has an impact, purpose, and powerful meaning. Line editing is making sure that the ideas and stories are presented to match the intention of the author while staying true to the author's tone and voice. This stage of the editing process is about polishing the prose that sits upon the strong structural foundation.

Copy Editing

After line editing comes the copy editing. Now is the time to look for all the spelling, grammar, word choice, and punctuation edits. This is what most people think of when they hear someone is a book editor. While that isn't wrong, hopefully, you can see that skipping straight to this stage of the editing journey cuts out some core and fundamental pieces that could heavily influence the success of your book. The best time to bring in a copy editor is when your manuscript is nearly finalized, and it's time to ensure that all the i's are dotted, and the t's are crossed. This step is critical to ensuring books are ready for submission and publication.

Proofreading

This is the last stage of the editing process. This is the final look. A proofreader will review the formatted manuscript to catch any mistakes that may have been missed during earlier editing stages. It is recommended to bring in a fresh pair of eyes for this stage to help catch any typos that may have been missed. This works best when the proofreader is a new person who hasn't read the manuscript yet. Many writers try to do this for themselves, and while it is possible, you have, at this stage, likely read your manuscript more times than you would like to admit. It can be very challenging to catch any last typos before you go to print, so asking for support here is a powerful last step in the editing process. Personally, I find that my brain won't catch typos or missing words because I know what I meant to say, so my brain fills in the intended words and doesn't consume what is actually on the page. That is why inviting someone else into the process at this stage is critical to having a finalized manuscript without typos.

Sensitivity Editors and Readers

Not all books require this step along the editing journey, but it is a very valuable one to mention here. Sensitivity editors provide feedback on cultural, ethnic, or marginalized representations within your manuscript. They ensure authenticity, accuracy, and sensitivity in portrayals. Consider hiring sensitivity readers if your manuscript features characters or themes outside of your own experiences, particularly if you're writing about marginalized communities. Again, this isn't required for all books, but it is worth knowing that this support and resource is available.

The editing process is made up of stages that do take time. But that doesn't mean it can't be a creative process in and of itself. No matter if you are planning to self-edit or work with professional editors, it's important to be honest with where your editing strengths lie. Taking a step back and consuming your work as a reader, not the creator, can be a challenge. This begins by taking some time away from your manuscript to come back with fresh eyes and to assess which areas of the editing process you feel you are strongest at. This doesn't mean you aren't a well-rounded author or don't have the skills to be published—it is very common! We have creative brains after all. This is just the part where leaning into professional help works to continue to mold and elevate your story for its greatest potential impact. For some authors, the structural changes are easy for them to spot, while for others, this can be the most challenging stage of the editing process. As I mentioned, proofreading is tough for me, so I will invite a proofreader into that stage of editing for my work—as was the case for this book.

While professional editors sometimes offer more than one service, it is important to ensure you know exactly what you are getting with key deliverables outlined prior to the start of your engagement. It is important to find the right partner for you and your book and not to rush each stage. Each step holds its own value in making your book the biggest success it can be. The needs of each manuscript are different. Finding the right editor for you is critical to making the editing process as smooth and engaging as possible.

Here are five key questions to ask a potential book editor to help ensure they're the right fit for you:

1. What experience do you have with my genre or type of book?

   This helps you understand if the editor has expertise in the genre's unique conventions and reader expectations.

2. Can you describe your editing style and approach?

   Some editors are more hands-on with suggestions, while others might focus on preserving the writer's voice. Knowing this will give insight into how well their style aligns with your needs.

3. What are your expectations of me as the author during the editing process?

   This sets clear expectations around communication, feedback, and revisions, and gives you a sense of their collaboration style.

4. How do you handle feedback or disagreements?

   Since editing can be subjective, it's helpful to know how the editor approaches differing opinions to ensure respectful and constructive collaboration.

5. Can you provide examples of previous work, a sample edit, or client testimonials?

   Seeing examples or hearing from an editor's previous clients can offer assurance about their editing skills, professionalism, and ability to deliver on expectations.

Additionally, many editors offer a sample edit to provide insight into their editing process and convey the types of feedback they will focus on.

The most important thing to remember is that while an editor is here to provide professional feedback, at the end of the day, this is your book! You get to make all final decisions about what gets changed and what doesn't. You should never feel pressured to make changes to your book that you are not on board with.

There may be times when you have to let go of how you thought your book was going to come to life. The writing and editing process is not linear and often asks us to create the path as we walk down it. This is a great time to revisit chapter 3, *On Doing Hard Things*. Are you experiencing grief in letting go of aspects of your story? Are you questioning yourself and wondering if anyone will want to read your book? The cultivation of your mindset, along with honoring the feelings that arise throughout the process, is just as important as the final words you select to place on the page.

Whether you choose to work with a professional editor or not, you will read your book a million times throughout the editing process. Here are my tips for creating a successful self-editing path:

- Take it slow and steady. You won't be able to edit at the same pace that you wrote. For example, if you had a writing goal of 500 words per writing session, you won't be able to edit 500 words in the same amount of time. Editing is slower because you're analyzing work already written instead of getting words on the page.

- Allow space. Take longer breaks to allow your brain to have more space between editing sessions. This way, you can come back to it with the freshest eyes possible.
- Editing isn't always about paring down; it can also be about adding words and concepts. Editing can involve writing more to expand on concepts while adding value through in-depth descriptions.
- Follow the editing flow laid out previously. Start with the bigger structural pieces and work your way through to proofreading.

Breaking down the editing process into steps is a powerful exercise that can help you feel less overwhelmed. Identify what you need to do first, second, and third based on the outlined editing stages above. This supports the editing process by breaking it down into manageable steps rather than tackling all structural and copy edits at once, for example. From there, you can create a timeline for completing your edits, much like you approached creating a writing practice. Remember that both the writing and editing processes are temporary—one day you'll have a completed book. As life changes and evolves, you'll only be writing and editing your book once, not forever. When it feels hard, remember that you are fulfilling a promise to yourself of having your dream book out in the world. Keep going.

How to Know When You're Done Editing

The editing process can feel endless. Knowing when your book is ready to be published can be a challenging inflection point and will differ from writer to writer. You could spend all the time in the world questioning if you used the right word in each sentence. You can reread the manuscript a thousand times and still find typos or cringe at your writing. There are best-selling books out there with typos—it happens. The aim here isn't perfection. Even authors who published books years ago will cringe when referencing previously published work because they have continued to grow in their writing skills with each piece of published work. A book is a snapshot in time of your life—reflective of who you were in the moment and your relationship to writing. There comes a point in your writing journey when it is time to share your story. The work is no longer yours; it belongs to your readers.

Just like an artist who hangs his paintings in a gallery, publishing a book means your work gets to be received, consumed, and admired by others. Knowing when to stop editing is personal, but most of the authors I've worked with reach a point where "good enough is good enough." Plus, there's often another story pulling at their heartstrings that needs to be written!

As you approach the end of the editing process, if you find you are just nitpicking at things, it's time to let it go. Let it be what it is and allow your book to emerge in the world so that it can inspire and transform the lives it needs to. Let your book meet its readers. And if that isn't enough to allow the book to be published, come back to your why and your Book Concept Statement. Have you fulfilled what you set out to do? If the answer is yes, then it is definitely time to share it with readers. You never know, it might just be their new favorite book!

The editing process is about bringing clarity and depth to your words. It is creating and shaping your book into the most impactful and elevated reader experience it can be. The key is to allow the editing journey to be a magical refinement process that shapes your book to its fullest potential. Done and good is better than never published.

Your Path to Publishing

Publishing a book is the goal for many writers. Your book isn't just for you. It is an avenue where your story gets to meet its readers and fulfills your desire to be a published author. Let's face it: becoming a published author is a bucket list item—it might be why you're reading this book. As you continue down your writing and editing journeys, you may begin to consider the publishing path you'd like to take. The publishing industry has been evolving, and many paths for publishing your book have emerged. For the longest time, traditional publishing was the only way to get your manuscript published. This requires getting an agent who submits your book to publishers who respond by saying "Yes" or "No" to paying you to publish your book. The idea of being paid an advance has been romanticized, and while it is exciting, it is important to read the fine print to ensure you're entering into the right partnership for your book. Remember that the advance must be earned back through book sales once your book is published, before you begin earning royalties.

Thankfully, we live in a time where additional avenues of publishing have emerged, such as hybrid and self-publishing. To help you decide which publishing path you want to proceed with, let's explore each path along with the pros and cons so you can make the best decision for your writing goals.

Traditional Publishing

This is the most well-known path to publishing. It is the longest-standing format that has been used to publish books since the printing press was invented. This path involves pitching your book to literary agents who then shop your book around to interested publishers. Think of book agents as the realtors of the book world. They help to broker deals and get you in front of the right buyers, AKA publishers. Rarely do traditional publishers accept book submissions directly from writers. This is why the traditional path to publishing has the longest timeline to bring your book to market. Patience and perseverance are required. Here is a breakdown of what the traditional publishing process looks like:

- *Querying Agents (6–12+ months):* Once your fiction manuscript is complete, this is the first step on the traditional publishing path. Start by writing a compelling query letter and researching agents who represent your genre. It may take several months (or rounds of submissions) to secure representation. This is where a lot of authors stop because rejection is a part of the process. Many agents I've spoken with receive more than 200 submissions a week. Not only do they not have the bandwidth to respond to every author, but they also don't get paid for that time. The literary agent business model works akin to a real estate agent—they only get paid when they sell a house. If they aren't selling books to a publisher, they aren't making money. Be patient, be consistent, and take a break if you need to. Your book holds value; don't forget that even when rejection feels endless.

- *Note:* For nonfiction authors, you'll need to create a book proposal with sample chapters to send to publishers prior to writing your book. This will also require putting together details on what your book is about, who it is for, etc. The reason nonfiction books don't need to be fully written prior to a publishing deal is that the advance often goes toward the time and resources needed to conduct research for the book.

- *Publisher Submission (6–12 months):* Once you have secured an agent, they will submit your manuscript to publishers. This is a time when patience will also be needed to allow your agent to represent you and find the right publisher for your book. This is a great time to start writing a new book and working on what marketing you can do to help build anticipation for your book release.

- *Production Timeline (12–24 months):* After a publisher accepts your book, they will handle editing, cover design, print production, and distribution to bookstores and libraries. Marketing support can vary, so building your author platform and starting marketing efforts before your book's release is a valuable investment of your time.

- *Cost for Traditional Publishing:* There are minimal upfront costs. However, it is recommended to invest in an editor to help get your manuscript to a place that agents can easily read and be immersed in your world. It is all about putting your best foot forward and having a strong first impression. Some agents may provide editorial feedback but won't do a deep dive because, again, this is unpaid time for them. The industry standard for agents is a 15 percent commission on earnings, and publishers may offer an advance ($1,000–$100,000+).

Based on what we have explored, here are some pros and cons of traditional publishing:

Pros of Traditional Publishing
- Professional editing, design, and often marketing support
- Access to wide distribution networks—hello, bookstores and libraries!

Cons of Traditional Publishing
- Long timelines (2–3 years or more)
- Limited creative control (Some publishers may have the final say in edits and book cover design. This is why reading the contract very closely is important.)
- Lower royalties (5–15 percent)

This is a great path if you are willing to be patient due to the longer production timeline. Another thing to consider on this path is that not all marketing will come from the publisher. I've been hearing more and more from traditionally published authors that publishers are looking for authors with an existing audience across digital channels, such as social media and email newsletters. If you decide on the traditional publishing route, know that it doesn't mean that marketing will be handled for you. There will be some effort required of you; after all, it is your book, and you'll want to connect with readers directly to see the impact it has.

A lot of writers want to pursue this path because of the potential for upfront advances. And while there are many stories of authors receiving six-figure advances, that is usually the exception and not the norm. Plus, those advances are not free money. They have to be earned back. It's very important to work with a lawyer to review the contract so that you are fully aware of the terms and conditions. With all that being said, this is a wonderful path that provides the support and resources of a publishing house for getting your book out into the world and in front of your ideal readers.

Self-Publishing

Self-publishing is another path for publishing your book—one that has become very popular thanks to the digital age. This path offers full creative control and allows you to bring your book to market quickly. It provides you with complete creative control, but that also means taking a more hands-on approach to publishing your book. Once you have written the book, there are a number of steps to take to see your book come to life in a short period of time. Here is a breakdown of what the self-publishing process looks like:

- *Production Timeline (2–5 months):* You'll need to hire professionals for editing, such as developmental, line, and copy editing. You may also choose to have beta readers provide feedback.
- *Book Design:* Creating the cover design and formatting the interior of your book are critical steps for publish-

ing platforms to accept your book. While design tools like Canva offer templates, you often don't retain the copyright to designs made on these platforms. This is why working with a book designer who specializes in book cover design is most helpful in retaining copyrights. For formatting your book, this ensures that your book has the right page layout for print and ebook. Many authors will do this themselves using a program called Atticus, but there are many book formatters that you can hire as well.

- *Publishing Platforms:* Selecting a book publishing platform like Amazon Kindle Direct Publishing (KDP), IngramSpark, or a similar platform gets your books into the hands of readers. The power of these services is the print-on-demand feature, so you don't have to pay to have an inventory of books printed. Within this step, you'll also need to file for copyright protection and an International Standard Book Number (ISBN). All books are required to be categorized using the ISBN.

- *Book Marketing:* The responsibility of marketing your book falls to you on the self-publishing path. Because of this, it is helpful to create a marketing plan that starts prior to your book launch to help build momentum.

- *Cost of Self-Publishing:* The cost of self-publishing can vary from $3,000–$12,000+ for editing, book cover design, formatting, copyright filing, purchasing an

ISBN, and marketing. A common misconception I hear about self-publishing is that it's free. That is not the case if you want to retain the copyrights and bring forward a polished book that readers love.

Based on what we have explored, here are some pros and cons of self-publishing:

<u>Pros of Self-Publishing</u>
- Full creative and timeline control
- Higher earnings (35–70 percent after print-on-demand fees)
- Direct connection to your audience

<u>Cons of Self-Publishing</u>
- Upfront financial investment
- Requires self-marketing
- Learning curve for publishing tools
- Fewer distribution channels

Self-publishing is an empowering path to getting your book into the world in a timeline that you control while retaining full creative control. With that being said, editing, marketing, and learning publishing tools can take up significant amounts of time. If you are entrepreneurially minded, get excited about learning new things, and want to retain full control of your book, then this path is a great one for you.

Hybrid Publishing

This path to publishing sounds exactly like its name: it combines aspects of both traditional and self-publishing. This is a great path for many authors, including nonfiction writers. What makes this path unique is that while it shares some of the upfront costs of self-publishing, it combines the team support and distribution channels of traditional publishing. The best place to start with this publishing path is to research the different hybrid publishers and find one that excels in your genre. Most hybrid publishers offer consultations and exploratory calls so that you can interview them to learn about their publishing process to ensure they align with your goals and vision. Here is a breakdown of what the hybrid publishing process looks like:

- *Collaboration with a Hybrid Publisher:* Writers pay for some services (book coaching, editing, and design) and receive professional support from their expert team.
- *More Creative Control:* Authors who work with a hybrid publisher have more creative control over the final edits made to their manuscript, as well as more input when it comes to cover design, than working with a traditional publisher.

- *Production Timeline (6–12 months):* The hybrid production timeline can be faster than traditional publishing but slower than self-publishing.
- *Cost of Hybrid Publishing:* The cost of hybrid publishing can vary from $5,000–$20,000. There are many factors that determine the pricing based on the publisher, editing support, and distribution plan.

Based on what we have explored, here are some pros and cons of hybrid publishing:

Pros of Hybrid Publishing
- Professional services with more control than traditional publishing.
- Access to distribution channels.
- Retain higher royalties compared to traditional publishing.

Cons of Hybrid Publishing
- High upfront costs.
- Variety in expertise (research hybrid publishers to ensure they publish books in your genre).
- Marketing support can be limited, and authors often need to play a big role in marketing their book.

The hybrid approach to publishing is a wonderful path that combines a number of the benefits from both traditional and self-publishing. In my experience, I see a lot of nonfiction writers take this path. That's not to say it isn't a great option for fiction writers, too, but the ability to have a publisher and a quicker timeline than traditional publishing can be very productive for entrepreneurs and thought leaders seeking to position themselves as experts within their fields.

Deciding Which Publishing Path Is Right for You

As you can see, each path to publishing comes with pros and cons. Ultimately, the path you choose will depend on your publishing goals. I recommend taking some time to research and weigh the pros and cons to help you decide which path is right for your writing project. I've created a few questions for you to reflect on to help you determine which path is right for you:

1. What are my publishing goals?
2. What do I want to experience? (Think about the team and support you'd like to have in place.)
3. What is an ideal timeline for publishing my book?
4. What budget do I have available?

Once you are clear on your publishing goals, conduct some research into each publishing option. If you know any other authors who have taken a publishing path that you are interested in, reach out to see if you can ask them questions about their experience. It can be beneficial to speak with authors who have worked with traditional or hybrid publishers to hear more about their experiences. The more insight you can gain, the more informed you will be about choosing the right path for your book. As you decide your publishing path, remember that each author's publishing path is unique, and success can only be determined by you.

Veronica, an author I worked with, is the perfect example of this. She chose a different path to publishing for each of her books, which is one of the great things about being a writer in this space and time. Just because you choose one path doesn't mean you can't change your mind the next time around. For her first book, Veronica landed a traditional publishing deal, which she had dreamed of since she was a young child. She was ecstatic to receive the advance and be introduced to her editing team. Over the course of twenty-four months, Veronica worked with her publisher to edit, market, and publish her book. Upon reflecting on the process, Veronica found that there had been some bumps in the road that deterred her from wanting to take this path again in the future. From editing decisions to cover design, Veronica felt the publisher was often pushing her to make decisions that she might not otherwise have made. Not to mention that the twenty-four-month process from the advance to the publishing date was a tiring one.

When it came to publishing her next book, Veronica decided to embark on self-publishing. This way, she could better control the timeline and decision-making process without having a team of people who encouraged her to do anything other than what she wanted to do. While she didn't have an advance to help cover the cost of editing or book cover design, she found it inspiring to collaborate with the service providers who best understood her vision. Veronica was able to shorten her path to publishing to twelve months by taking the self-publishing route.

I share Veronica's story because there are pros and cons to each path. One is not better than the other. It all comes down to your goals, timeline, and budget. Veronica was successful with both book launches, and her readers loved both books.

Publishing is the culmination of your writing journey. To make your book the success you want it to be, it's important to consider each path to publishing and mindfully select the one that is the best fit for you and your book. And, if you plan to write multiple books, the great news is that just because you chose one path for your first book doesn't mean you have to take that same publishing path for your next book. You can choose different paths based on what you and your current book need.

At this stage, I like to ask authors to revisit their why statement for writing their book. As you embark on the publishing journey, it can be helpful to tap back into your intention for writing your book, which can act as a filter to help you decide which publishing path is right for you. Being mindful in the publishing journey is just as important as being mindful in the writing journey. It can be easy to get caught up in the list of to-dos and worrying about who is going to buy your book. When we get stuck in the doing, it is usually a signal that we've moved away from our truest intentions and our egos are driving the train. If you find this is the case, take a step back, breathe, and revisit your why. Settle back into your intentions and then act from that place.

No matter which path to publishing you choose, bringing your book into the world is a powerful act of courage.

Mindful Marketing for Authors

Marketing is storytelling and—as an author—you already know how to do that. No matter which publishing path you take, marketing yourself and your book will be a part of bringing your book forward into the world. If you're feeling icky even reading the word *marketing* because it conjures up the image of a slimy salesman, I get it. Marketing is the process of letting people know that you have something to offer. It is like waving your hands in the air, saying, "Hey, I've got a cool story to tell you." As a result, it allows the people who want to hear that story to step forward. You've taken the time to write a book with intention that offers to provide positive impact and inspiration—there is nothing slimy about that!

Many authors are afraid of marketing because it requires them to step out from behind the pages and present themselves alongside their work. Being seen can be scary. But here is the thing, marketing doesn't have to feel forced or uncomfortable when you align it with your values. The even better news is that marketing is a vast umbrella term that can cover everything from public relations to social media, and you don't have to do it all. It's about mindfully selecting what will work best for you.

By understanding what marketing will work best for you and aligns with your values, you can pick the marketing activities that allow you to enjoy showing up in those spaces and remain consistent. Most people need to see something upwards of twelve times before they even consider buying. I've seen many authors stop talking about their book for fear of sounding repetitive and annoying—that's not the case! Attention spans have shrunk, and all of us are inundated with messaging every day. Remaining consistent and sharing about your book is how you break through that noise and connect with your readers.

The goal of marketing your book starts with your intention. It is about creating a holistic approach that supports you and your goals over time. The purpose of marketing is to accomplish your goals for total book sales while building a loyal community of readers. Marketing is a journey and doesn't happen overnight. There is no such thing as an overnight success. It might look like that is happening for other people, but those overnight successes are often the result of multiple planned marketing campaigns. The key to successful marketing is consistency. Showing up and putting words on the page during each writing session builds toward a completed book, and the same is true for marketing. Every effort builds upon another, over time. That's why taking a holistic approach that considers all aspects of who you are, your goals, and who your readers are helps to create a sustainable plan that doesn't burn you out. The key is to create a marketing plan that supports your goals for years to come while connecting and inspiring readers.

Define Your Ideal Reader

Not everyone is your audience. Sorry, not sorry. Even if your book has a mass appeal, there is still a segment of the readership that will be pulled more toward your story and genre. Having a sense of who your ideal reader is will help you refine the spaces you need to be showing up and marketing in. For example, if you are a romance writer, your ideal readers are likely visiting local romance bookstores, are members of online communities that discuss romance novels, or go to romance book events and conferences. Understanding your ideal readership will help you tailor your marketing efforts to reach readers more effectively. When it comes to marketing, there is nothing more discouraging than showing up in a space that isn't a match for you and feeling like a failure. You have to make sure you're in the right rooms to begin with.

Before you start marketing your book, it's crucial to identify who you want to read your book. To do that, consider the following questions:

- How would I describe my ideal reader?
- What are their interests?
- Where do they hang out online?
- Where do they hang out offline?
- Why do they have an interest in my story's topic, theme, or genre?

As you gain clarity around your ideal reader, it doesn't have to be a detailed demographic profile of their income, age, and location—unless that is helpful. Understanding your ideal reader can be as simple as defining your audience as "women who love a good love story," or "This book is for spiritual entrepreneurs." If you don't know all the answers to the questions above, that is okay too. It might be helpful to do some research and ask other authors in your genre what has worked for them. As you begin to market your book, you'll start to refine the answers to these questions based on the traction you gain—or don't—based on the wins you receive.

Build an Author Platform

Your author platform is the hub of who you are and your books. Your author platform is made up of your bio, your books, your book's message, and your on and offline presence. Essentially, it is the story you want to tell about yourself and your book. It is the messaging you put forth to guide people's perceptions of you. An author platform is the answer to this question: If you released a book tomorrow, who would know about it—and why would they care? In other words, your author platform is how you establish a connection with your readers.

Your ideal audience wants to know who you are as a writer and *why* you wrote your book. On the flip side, your author platform also establishes who your book is *not* for. Building a strong author platform will help you establish your brand and expand your reach to the right people. Building your author brand hub might look like creating an author website that speaks to who you are as an author, why you write, and why you wrote the book that you did. This messaging can then be extended to social media profiles, blog posts, newsletters, and events.

Readers not only love books, but they also love the story behind the person who chose to write this story. You don't have to share every detail of your life, but your audience will love getting to know the person who wrote the story and your process. When they hear in your own words why it matters to you, they feel compelled to buy your book—that's why I say marketing is storytelling too. Your author platform is the story you are telling ideal readers that moves them into the action of buying your book. To help you think about the principles of your author brand, ask yourself these questions:

- How do I want to be known as an author?
- What aspects of the why behind my book am I comfortable sharing?
- What aspects of my life and writing process am I comfortable sharing?
- What aspects of my life and writing process am I *not* comfortable sharing?
- What do I want people to know about me as an author?

When you become clear on your author brand, you become clear on how you want to show up and talk about your book. This is what it means to align your marketing with your values to reach readers who are going to be your biggest fans. When you are clear on what stage you're standing on and how you want to talk to audiences, then you can begin to show up in the right spaces and not feel like you're yelling at an empty room.

Develop a Compelling Book Cover and Book Blurb

As you gain clarity around your author platform and the story you are crafting around yourself, two important parts of your marketing are your book blurb and book cover. These are critical marketing tools to invest in for the professional presentation of your book because these are your audience's first impressions of your book. A book blurb (also called a book description) is the short, enticing summary of your book that appears on the back cover, online product pages (like Amazon), or in marketing materials. Its sole purpose is to hook the reader and convince them to buy your book. This text can also be used on your website and to help frame how you talk about your book. Many of the authors I work with find that the writing of the book blurb is the hardest part. How do you boil down compelling aspects of your book into a captivating paragraph?!

A great book blurb is typically 150–250 words and conveys just enough about the plot or subject matter. Think of this as the TV commercial for your book. It doesn't give everything away, but it makes readers curious enough to buy your book.

A professional book cover visually represents your book's genre and captures readers' attention. I can't be the only one who feels like the book cover is the hardest part of the publishing journey! The pressure to have a cover that is "just right" is very real. What has helped me is to focus on the most important elements. This means having a title that is clear and easy to read. This also means looking at other books in my genre to see what elements I like and don't like. Creating a Pinterest board of inspiration can be helpful not only for you to understand what you like and why, but you can also share this with your book designer.

Take the time to create a first impression that is aligned with your intention for your book. Don't rush this process! Make your first impression count because people do choose to read a book by its cover.

Select Your Marketing Avenues

As you gain clarity around your ideal readers, develop your author platform, design a book cover, and write a book blurb, it's time to think about where you will be marketing your book. In other words, which avenue or marketing channels do you want to direct your message to? Think of a marketing channel or avenue as a highway where readers are zooming about in their cars. You decide which streets you want to establish billboards on. Here are some different avenues to choose from:

Leverage Social Media

A popular form of a "billboard" for book marketing is social media. That doesn't mean it is for everyone. If you hate social media and detest the idea of having to be in these spaces, then don't use them. But if you're willing to be in these spaces, social media can be a powerful marketing tool for authors. Utilize platforms such as YouTube, Facebook, Instagram, TikTok, Goodreads, and Storygraph to connect with readers, share updates, post engaging content, and run promotions or giveaways. Engage with your audience, respond to comments, and build relationships with your readers.

The more you can have fun with creating content on social media, the more the audience can feel that. After all, the word *social* is in its name. The key to social media is—you guessed it—consistently being social, along with being strategic about the types of content you share. I recommend picking three to four content themes to post about regularly. For example, one content theme might focus on your writing process, another on books you love, while another could focus on asking people to join your newsletter or buy your book, with the final area of focus being what inspires you as a writer. A lot of social media is testing to understand what resonates with people on different platforms. If you don't find your readers on one, then move to the next. You do not need to be in all places at once.

Utilize Book Bloggers and Book Reviewers

Another marketing channel to consider is book bloggers and book reviewers. These individuals already have an engaged audience and can help generate buzz for your book. Research and connect with bloggers and reviewers who cater to your book's genre and offer them a (sometimes free) copy of your book in exchange for an honest review. Positive reviews can boost your book's credibility and attract more readers. Be sure to do your research and use your discernment to make sure you're working with reputable reviewers and don't fall victim to any scammers out there. If something feels off, trust that.

Host Virtual Events and Book Launches

Hosting book events either online or in-person can be a powerful way to connect directly with readers. When we can share spaces together, we connect on a deeper level than we do with just a social media post alone. Consider what conferences you can speak at, bookstores you can do a reading at, or virtual events you can host to help you connect with readers from all over the world. I have found that many readers feel like they are meeting a celebrity when they meet the authors of their favorite books. I know I've felt that way!

If this terrifies you, I get it. It took me *years* of practice before I was more comfortable with public speaking. I say "more comfortable" because I still get nervous. What has helped me is to tap into the exciting feelings I experience post-events. I always feel energized and more connected to a community of book lovers after a book event. If this feels uncomfortable to you, I invite you to try it! There is beauty when we step outside of our comfort zones, especially when a group of book lovers get together.

Utilize Email Marketing

Email marketing is not dead! Building a list of people who have opted in to receive updates and news from you is one of the most powerful marketing tools. The best part? You own your list. Unlike a social media following, which could disappear tomorrow if the platform were to shut down, an email list is yours to retain. Building an email list is a valuable marketing strategy for authors. This can be a central piece of your author platform, inviting readers in with a free chapter or exclusive content in exchange for their email addresses. It is important to note that you need to use an email marketing platform such as Mailchimp or Kit to send communications. It is illegal to add people to your marketing email list from your personal email and to send emails to someone who hasn't opted in. Meaning, they need to have consented to receive marketing emails either directly on your website or through a sign-up sheet. Once someone has signed up, you can send writing and event updates along with promotional offers to your subscribers. Email marketing is one of the best ways to connect with your biggest fans.

Offer Limited-Time Promotions and Bundles

Offering limited-time promotions or book bundles (if you have more than one book) can create a sense of urgency and drive sales. Offering discounts on your book or running a promotional giveaway during book launch or holiday seasons can attract readers. My caveat here is to use discounts sparingly. The more discounts you offer, the more people will come to expect them. This means your audience won't buy your book at full price and will just wait until your next promotion. This creates a cycle of you creating one discount after another to make sales.

With that being said, discounts can create urgency to motivate readers to buy now. I've also seen authors come together and create a bundle with their books and split the profits so they can tap into each other's audience. This is a marketing avenue you can consider and test out. See what happens and then decide if you want to do it again.

Seek Out Book Awards and Literary Competitions

Winning book awards or literary competitions can boost your book's visibility and credibility. There are a lot of organizations that run annual book awards. In fact, I'm a book judge for a couple of organizations as a way of giving back to the writing community. It brings me a lot of joy to see powerful writing rewarded—but remember, the act of publishing a book is a reward itself! A third-party award is just the icing on the cake.

Do your research for organizations and submit your book to relevant awards and competitions in your genre or niche, and then use the accolades to promote your book in your marketing efforts.

Collaborate with Other Authors or Influencers

Collaborating with other authors or influencers in your genre can expand your reach and introduce your book to new audiences. Consider hosting joint events, cross-promoting each other's books, or participating in collaborative blog posts or social media campaigns. Attending conferences and writing retreats can be a powerful way to build relationships with like-minded authors.

By choosing the marketing avenues that work best for you, you can begin to experiment to see what starts to generate momentum, then keep doing that. Marketing doesn't have to be this nebulous and confusing thing. If in this process, the fear of being seen starts to crop up, that is okay. As authors, it can be challenging to step out beyond the page. By taking the time to create a marketing plan that supports you and your values, this fear can begin to soften. This is also a great place to check in with your why for writing your book. After all, FEAR stands for False Evidence Appearing Real. Fear is a feeling state that thrives when we continue to feed it with negative thoughts, worst-case scenario thinking, or seek additional evidence to prove it right. As someone who has personally been victimized by fear a number of times in my life, it's amazing how quickly a doom spiral can take place. If and when fear does show up, remember to breathe. Check back in with your why and remember that you are growing and expanding as an author. Marketing your book is a new way of expanding. The fear of things not working out or not getting the results you desire is very common. You get to assess and choose what needs to be true for you.

Mindful marketing is created from being authentic to who you are and establishing a holistic approach that doesn't burn you out while providing a way for you to share your story with the world and connect with readers who are yearning for your story. Your book won't be for everyone—that's okay. Your book will connect with the readers it is meant to.

By adapting a test-and-learn mindset and leaning into your natural storytelling abilities, you can select the marketing channels that best support your efforts and remain consistent and persistent. Even toilet paper brands still spend millions of dollars annually on advertising for a product we use every day. People need to be consistently reminded of what is available to them and the value it offers. It takes time to build traction—remember, there are no overnight successes! Be kind to yourself in this process. Your readers are waiting to hear your story.

Your Book, Your Legacy

Your book is more than words—it's your legacy. Your story has a powerful message to share. Your book can transcend the space and time it was written in. It can live on well beyond your beautiful years on this planet. The themes and messages within your book have the power to invite readers to reflect on areas within their own lives or tap into emotions and possibilities in a new way. The message within your book can continue to live on and meet readers exactly where they are, at a time they need to read it.

The journey of being a writer is one of many layers. When we can honor this journey, the more we can tap into our authentic voice to share our message powerfully. By connecting to your truest essence and combining it with many universal human emotions, you can translate those feelings onto the page. The words you write not only entertain readers but also make them feel a deeper meaning as it relates to their own lives.

Embracing the writing journey means that our initial idea for our book is rarely where we end up. That is also a part of the process. It doesn't mean you did it wrong. It means you did it right. You allowed the writing to be what it needed to be to unfold. Using the written word to express your story is not only an act of courage, but it is a way to create your legacy. That is why taking a mindful approach to writing means knowing when to slow down, when to learn, when to write, and when to take a break. Writing an impactful book isn't found in doing more; rather, it is found in listening to your true intention and allowing the heart of your story to shine through.

As we take a mindful approach to writing, we not only support our own personal growth in skills and mindset, but our words can have more depth on the page. That is the power of storytelling—it's healing for the author and the reader. A book has a powerful way of holding a larger purpose, which creates a ripple effect far beyond the page.

While your writing journey may ebb and flow, my hope is that after reading this book, you will feel more confident embarking on this journey knowing that you are not alone, foolish, or a terrible writer. You're exactly where you need to be. Writing a book is no small feat—but it is doable, especially when your intention is clear. The writing process asks that you expand your knowledge, integrate what you learn, and engage in introspection. You can write a book. And you'll enjoy the process a lot more when you can take a more mindful and intentional journey. You're learning, growing, and expanding as you bring forward your life's work. Your self-worth is not determined by how much you pushed through the writing process. However long it takes to write your book is the time it takes.

Your success as a writer is not determined by the number of bestseller lists your name rises to the top of or by how much money you make from book sales. Your success is defined by having finished writing a book that your soul called you to write. Don't compare your journey to anyone else's. Your success is that you did something challenging that most people want to do but never finish or even start—celebrate that!

Writing isn't just about putting words on the page; it is about our own expansion as people who develop a deep belief in what is possible for ourselves and our writing, as well as being a perpetual student in order to write books that inspire and have a positive impact on readers. If you find that resistance is showing up either in the form of beliefs or from a lack of knowledge, trust yourself and connect with the layers that make you *you.*

There is no one-size-fits-all for taking a mindful and intentional approach to writing your book. The more you can find and honor your own process, the more your book will come to life with light and positive impact that comes through on the page, making it even more purposeful for the reader. It will be honest, real, and authentic to you. Trust your creative process if you feel stuck. Focus on this question: what is the light that will come through your words?

I hope that you celebrate your writing journey. Not just at the fabulous book launch party I know you're going to throw on your publication day, but for completing every step along the way. Celebrating is how we show up for ourselves and acknowledge every step we take down the path to accomplishing our goals. When we celebrate, we help to build momentum. The writing journey unfolds over time and asks you to reactively walk down the path even when your feet are tired.

The intention behind creating your book and your why for writing will be felt by readers. By taking a mindful approach to writing your book, you have not only created a joyful journey for yourself, but your readers will be able to tell (even subconsciously) that your reason for bringing this book forward has a ripple effect that can be felt well beyond the page. That is the powerful legacy that this world needs.

Many of the authors I've mentioned in this book came to writing from many different paths, but all of them found meaning in completing their books. From the writer who transferred their grief into a moving novel, to Martha who overcame their fear of failure, to Lauri who worked past her self-judgment to find her voice—all these writers found meaning well beyond the completed book.

The satisfaction that comes with reaching the end of a completed manuscript can feel like a renewed beginning. You're embarking on a new era of being a writer, and the path you've walked down might have been windy, but no one truly knows the richness of the journey other than you. You've developed a deeper connection with yourself while bringing your dream book into reality. That is something to be proud of.

Summer is my favorite season, and I'm always in awe of all the flowers in bloom. We always look at the flower with its colorful petals and stick our noses in it to enjoy its floral scent, and we often ignore the stem, seed, and root system. I mean, they don't exactly evoke the same beauty as the petals do. But the thing is, the flower wouldn't exist without the seed that sprouted the root system, which then grew its stem for the beautiful flower to rest upon. The whole system works together to keep itself nourished and thriving. A book's purpose and outline are like a flower's stem. It is the support structure—the spine connecting messages and transporting nutrients. Your story begins with a seed, sprouts roots, and an outline helps guide you to a beautiful, floral, and happy ending. It's not just about the result of being productive, but it's about how you feel while creating something that holds meaning.

At the beginning of this book, I shared how 81 percent of people want to write a book, but very few finish.[15] Now that you have read this book, you have what it takes to ensure that you are a writer who *actually* finishes writing your book. At this stage, you are already more likely to finish writing your book than others who haven't taken the time to define their writing goals and identify a path for reaching them. The key is that only you can give meaning to your writing, but I promise that if you take a mindful and intentional approach to writing, you will not only surprise and delight yourself, but your readers will feel deeply connected to the words you write. Trust that all the words that you needed to express have landed on the page.

Together, we have explored why your intent matters. We've gotten to the heart of your story, we've explored what it means to write from your truth with mindfulness, and we've paved the path for what is to come once you've completed your first draft manuscript with editing, publishing, and marketing.

You know that the secret to writing an impactful book isn't about forcing yourself to sit down and write, but it is about tapping into your why and inviting the creative process to show you what it is you need to learn in order to have the success you desire. Writing is a channel for finding our way home to ourselves. The path is often created as we start to walk down it. Waiting around for the perfect timing or circumstances will never happen; you have to create it. Allow the unfolding of the writing journey to express your creativity on your own terms, unapologetically.

A good book is defined by how readers feel after reaching the last page of your book. I know you're going to leave them with a wonderful feeling. When we can make space for our mind, body, and soul to write our story, we tap into wisdom that is deeper than our logical mind. Let's celebrate the work you have done in exploring a writing practice that nurtures you toward "The End." Here is to leaving an impact on the world and inspiring readers. Here is to no longer telling our stories to be quiet but boldly letting them take center stage. Here is to you, dear writer, for being brave enough to share your voice, your story, and expand into the writer you were meant to become. Congratulations. No matter where your writing leads you, know that you've got this and I'm cheering you on every step of the way!

It is a true honor to be your guide and to witness powerful stories coming to life. Every book leaves a mark on the world. I look forward to seeing what positive imprint your book leaves. Your story matters. You've got this.

Resources

To further support your writing journey, a list of resources is provided below. I invite you to explore HerNarrative.com for access to informative blog posts, writing tools and courses, writing services, and more!

Free Tools:
- Word Count Tracker: https://www.hernarrative.com/word-count-tracker
- First Chapter Checklist: https://www.hernarrative.com/first-chapter-checklist
- Nonfiction Chapter Template: https://hernarrative.com/non-fiction-chapter-template
- Her Narrative Blog: https://www.hernarrative.com/blog

Courses:
- Idea to Manuscript: https://www.hernarrative.com/idea-to-manuscript
- Crafting Your Novel: Essential Foundations for Fiction Writers: https://www.hernarrative.com/crafting-your-novel
- Mapping Your Nonfiction Book: http://hernarrative.com/mapping-your-nonfiction-book

To learn more about Book Coaching and Developmental Editing services, visit https://www.hernarrative.com/write-a-book.

Subscribe on YouTube:

https://www.youtube.com/@hernarrative

Everything you need to support
your writing journey—scan the QR
code to explore all the resources!

Acknowledgements

This book wouldn't have been possible without the many writers who have crossed my path. Thank you to each and every author who has bravely embarked on the writing journey while being open and vulnerable in the process. Thank you for sharing your journey and letting me see beyond the words on the page.

Thank you to the amazing beta readers who helped shape this book: Sujata, Patricia, Lorin, Gloria, and Eliza. Your time and feedback were invaluable in helping bring this book forward.

Thank you to my editor, Shelby Harbour. Your advice and guidance helped ensure every T was crossed and every I was dotted.

Thank you to Jennifer Birge for the beautiful book cover design. You perfectly captured my vision while creating a welcome mat for readers to enter my world.

Thank you to the authors in the Book Magic program, for without you, this book would have remained inside my head for too long. Thank you for inspiring me to take the leap and finally put pen to paper.

About the Author

Charlotte Chipperfield is a book coach, developmental editor, and women's fiction writer passionate about helping writers bring their stories to life. She is the founder of Her Narrative, a writer education, book coaching, and editing company that empowers women to write unapologetically and share their truth with clarity, confidence, and intention. Charlotte is passionate about helping writers move through creative blocks and reconnect with their voice so they can share their truth on the page.

Charlotte is the author of *Write with Intention: A Mindful Journey to Writing Your Book*, born from her deep commitment to helping writers turn their ideas into meaningful, finished work. She is also a co-author of the anthology *Soul Rising: Guidance for Navigating Your Spiritual Awakening*, an anthology of personal essays exploring spiritual growth and transformation. When she's not writing or coaching, you'll find her learning languages, exploring new countries, or dreaming up her next retreat for writers.

Endnotes

1. Joseph Epstein, "Think You Have a Book in You? Think Again," *The New York Times*, September 28, 2002, https://www.nytimes.com/2002/09/28/opinion/think-you-have-a-book-in-you-think-again.html.

2. *"First Intention,"* in *Taber's Cyclopedic Medical Dictionary*, 24th ed., accessed May 30, 2025, https://www.tabers.com/tabersonline/view/Tabers-Dictionary/752053/all/first_intention.

3. Elizabeth L. Eisenstein, *The Printing Press as an Agent of Change* (Cambridge University Press, 1980).

4. Michael A. Singer, *The Untethered Soul: The Journey Beyond Yourself* (New Harbinger Publications, 2007).

5. Brianna Wiest, *The Pivot Year: 365 Days to Become the Person You Truly Want to Be* (Thought Catalog Books, 2023).

6. Jeannette Walls, *The Glass Castle: A Memoir* (Scribner, 2005).

7. Emily Henry, *Book Lovers* (Berkley, 2022).

8. Lauren Parvizi, *La Vie, According to Rose* (Lake Union Publishing, 2023).

9. Lisa Cron, *Wired for Story: The Writer's Guide to Using Brain Science to Hook Readers from the Very First Sentence* (Ten Speed Press, 2012).

10. Gertrude Chandler Warner, *The Boxcar Children* series (Albert Whitman, 1942–2023)

11. Steven Pressfield, *The War of Art: Break Through the Blocks and Win Your Inner Creative Battles* (Black Irish Entertainment, 2002).

12. Lisa Cron, *Wired for Story: The Writer's Guide to Using Brain Science to Hook Readers from the Very First Sentence* (Ten Speed Press, 2012).

13. Erica Harrison, "Finding Your 'Why': The Science Behind Value-Based Goal-Setting," Yoga Medicine, accessed May 30, 2025, https://yogamedicine.com/finding-your-why-the-science-behind-value-based-goal-setting.

14. William Moulton Marston, *Wonder Woman #1* (DC Comics, 1942).

15. Joseph Epstein, "Think You Have a Book in You? Think Again," *The New York Times*, September 28, 2002, https://www.nytimes.com/2002/09/28/opinion/think-you-have-a-book-in-you-think-again.html.

www.ingramcontent.com/pod-product-compliance
Lightning Source LLC
Chambersburg PA
CBHW060420130626
46555CB00005B/2153